THE PRODUCERS:
CONTEMPORARY CURATORS IN CONVERSATION
(5)

Also available in the B.READ series:

B.READ / ONE
NEW SITES – NEW ART
Tuula Arkio, Jan Debbaut, David Elliott, Christian Jabornegg,
Peter Jenkinson, András Pálffy, Dominic Williams

B.READ / TWO
THE PRODUCERS:
CONTEMPORARY CURATORS IN CONVERSATION
James Lingwood & Sune Nordgren
Clive Phillpot & Matthew Higgs

B.READ / THREE
ARTISTS AT WORK
Daniel Birnbaum, Lynne Cooke, Kathryn Kanjo,
Friedrich Meschede, Richard Wentworth

B.READ / FOUR
THE PRODUCERS:
CONTEMPORARY CURATORS IN CONVERSATION
(2)
Gilane Tawadros & Hans Ulrich Obrist
Frances Morris & Charles Esche
Guy Brett & Deanna Petherbridge

B.READ / FIVE
THE PRODUCERS:
CONTEMPORARY CURATORS IN CONVERSATION
(3)
Sharon Kivland & Adam Szymczyk
Ralph Rugoff & Richard Grayson
Lisa Corrin & Jon Bewley

B.READ / SIX
CURATING NEW MEDIA
Tamas Banovich; Sarah Cook; Vuk Cosic; Matthew Gansallo;
Karen Guthrie & Nina Pope; Iliyana Nedkova; Sune Nordgren;
Julian Stallabrass; Jon Thomson & Alison Craighead

B.READ / SEVEN
THE PRODUCERS:
CONTEMPORARY CURATORS IN CONVERSATION
(5)
Carolyn Christov-Bakargiev & Liam Gillick
Ute Meta Bauer & Mark Nash
Jeremy Millar & Teresa Gleadowe

The Producers: Contemporary Curators in Conversation (5)

A series of public events, sponsored jointly by the Department of Fine Art, University of Newcastle and BALTIC, The Centre for Contemporary Art. The series is organised by Professor Susan Hiller, BALTIC Chair in Contemporary Art, and Vicki Lewis, BALTIC curator, and is held in the fine art lecture theatre at the University. Members of the public and the University are warmly invited to attend.

Edited by Susan Hiller and Sarah Martin

First published in 2002 by BALTIC in collaboration with the
University of Newcastle, Department of Fine Art.

BALTIC
South Shore Road
Gateshead NE8 3BA
www.balticmill.com
ISBN 1-903655-13-7

University of Newcastle
Newcastle upon Tyne
NE1 7RU
ISBN 0-7017-0150

Printed and bound in Great Britain by Cox and Wyman Ltd.,
Cardiff Road, Reading, Berkshire.

Distributed by Cornerhouse Publications Ltd., 70 Oxford Street, Manchester M1 5NH

ACKNOWLEDGMENTS

The publishing team and the organisers of this series would like to thank everyone who helped to make the events run smoothly, in particular Volker Eichelmann, Lecturer in Fine Art at the University and Dave Pipkin, sound engineer. Special thanks also to Angela Horn and Wendy Lothian for their help with the transcripts.

This collection of curatorial conversations is the fifth publication documenting a series of events at the University of Newcastle. 'The Producers' series is organised jointly by the Department of Fine Art at the University and BALTIC, Gateshead. Since its inception in March 2000, it has contributed to expanding the context for contemporary art in the North East by bringing distinguished curators together to discuss their approaches to exhibition making. Interest in these conversations to date has exceeded the original ambition of Andrew Burton (Chair of the Department of Fine Art), Vicki Lewis (BALTIC curator) and myself. We hope that by collecting the transcripts together, many more people will be able to enjoy what has been a memorable series of public debates. The conversations in the current volume are the last in the series to be held at the University of Newcastle. Future 'Producers' events will be hosted by BALTIC in their newly-inaugurated premises.

SUSAN HILLER

The Producers: Contemporary Curators in Conversation (5)

CONTENTS

THE PRODUCERS: CONTEMPORARY CURATORS IN CONVERSATION

16 JANUARY 2002, UNIVERSITY OF NEWCASTLE, DEPARTMENT OF FINE ART

ANDREW RENTON AND SACHA CRADDOCK IN CONVERSATION CHAIRED BY PROF. JOHN MILNER

SUSAN HILLER:

Welcome to all of you. This is the first event in the fifth series of 'Producers' discussions between distinguished curators which, as you probably know, is a series of events initiated and sponsored collaboratively between the new BALTIC Centre for Contemporary Art in Gateshead and the Department of Fine Art here at the University of Newcastle. I'd like to take this opportunity to thank emphatically absolutely everyone who has helped to make these events and the subsequent publications run smoothly. I also want to acknowledge the commitment and interest of our audiences, whose close attention, combined with the probing questions and a fairly unique atmosphere of good will and good humour, have made these events extremely enjoyable – and that's thanks to all of you, as well as to the speakers, of course.

Today's conversation promises to be as stimulating and entertaining as the others. Our two speakers have very different backgrounds and take quite different approaches to their curatorial and critical projects, yet similarities may well emerge in the course of discussion.

I'd like to introduce them both to you briefly. Sacha Craddock is an independent art critic and lecturer who reviews contemporary art for newspapers such as *The Times* as well as for many art magazines and journals. She's also the author of numerous distinguished catalogue essays. Sacha has been a recent selector for the Turner Prize but I think she is possibly best known as the chair of 'New Contemporaries', which is the most important open exhibition for emerging artists in the U.K.

Andrew Renton is an independent curator and writer who has curated several major international exhibitions such as 'Manifesta' in Rotterdam, 'Browser' in Vancouver and Tate Modern, and most recently, 'Total Object Complete with Missing Parts' at Tramway in Glasgow. He has also published critical essays on aspects of contemporary art.

The chair today is Dr John Milner, who is well known to many of you as Professor of Art History at this university. He is the author of a number of distinguished art historical studies including *Kazimir Malevich and the Art of Geometry*, *A Dictionary of Russian and Soviet Artists* and most recently, *The Art of the Paris Commune*. Over to you John.

JOHN MILNER:

Thank you very much. We're going to try to get more time for questions from the floor today, but obviously the priority goes to our speakers so we shall see how we get on. Please feel invited to ask questions as the format of our discussion enters that phase. The usual format – Andrew will speak for fifteen minutes or so, followed by Sacha. Then there will be some discussion between them and then we will open it up to questions from the floor. Their careers alone, quite apart from what they say, must breed a lot of questions in your minds already, I should think. So, Andrew.

ANDREW RENTON:

Thank you. I'm delighted to be here. I'm an enormous fan of Newcastle and very excited to be associated in any way with the development of BALTIC. As a northerner, I feel extremely strongly that location is a key issue and it's something that I want to talk about in terms of some of the projects that I've worked on. I'm going to whizz through this, so that hopefully we can get a chance to talk in a more relaxed way thereafter.

What is it a curator does? I don't think anyone really knows what a curator does. The new notion of a curator is evolving – it's changing and lacks a precise definition. Two thoughts: have you ever been in a hotel with a partner and you're going down for breakfast and you're on the twentieth floor, and you ding the bell for the lift, it comes up and your partner is still in the room and so you try and keep the door open? The thing about trying to keep the door open is that there's two ways to do it. You can either keep the door open with that thing that says 'door open', or you can try to hold it open physically. At the same time, there's a guy down on the ground floor who's dinging the bell and he wants that lift to come down to the bottom of the building, so there's pressure on. Now, when that's happening, you're trying to resist and your job at that point is to try to keep that door open for as long as possible. If you just force it open you know it breaks – it makes that funny kind of crunching noise that you know is not healthy. As a curator, I think one's job is to hold that space open for as long as possible. It's always trying to close in, to fill itself with stuff, and your job is to make a space available for an artist to work and to develop all sorts of relations in that space, which at the same time is always closing down.

Another hotel metaphor – I do a lot of hotels – but this one is the thing that you did when you were a little kid and you went on your first holiday with your family. You arrive in the hotel and you're so excited. You're in the lobby checking in and you can't believe it, everything's there: there's that palm tree and the sofa's here and there's muzak and whatever. So you're looking, you're taking stock. Then you go and have your holiday – you fall in love, have a great week and check out a week later. You're checking out, you're in the same lobby and you look around: every single object is in the same place. Nothing's moved. They've only got one muzak tape, so it's just going round in circles; the palm tree isn't real anyway, it's actually plastic, so that hasn't even grown. Everything is as it was. And guess what? It looks different. Do you remember that feeling? Why does it look different? Because as an object, or as a series of objects in a space, it's transformed by your experience over time. I think that's one of the things that a curator does. To try to develop relationships between objects, artists and audiences, and to try and figure out how that changes and evolves.

That's part of the reason behind the show 'Total Object Complete with Missing Parts'. As a curator I've always had a problem with objects. We'll discuss that later. But I'm quite interested in the way that objects are and are not necessary for the artist to participate with in the work. Very often for me, the central issue in terms of curating a show is location. Where is it? What kind of space is it? This slide shows Tramway in Glasgow – a fantastic space which seems to generate work within it precisely because of the scale of the thing. That's one kind of space, but then it's also a question of 'where'. Where do we find ourselves? In what part of the world do we find ourselves? Why does this work travel well from one place to another? I'm thinking, for example, of this work by Eugenio Dittborn. Dittborn is an artist who works in Chile and twenty years ago, when he was trying to participate internationally, the only way to do things was to send his paintings by airmail in envelopes. They come out unfolded from one place to another and those envelopes bear witness to the journey that that painting made over the years, from one exhibition to another.

I'm just throwing things out here in terms of this particular show to give you a sense of the kind and the scale of things that can go on. This slide looks like the show's not ready yet, but no, it's a work by Nedko Solakov, who instructed two decorators to paint a 43-metre long wall, all day, every day, for the duration of the show, one painting the wall black, the other painting the wall white. It's about understanding where you are and about developing a relationship with the space, a relationship with the people who come and see that space. I'm very interested in artists who do that. I'm very interested in artists who take responsibility for where they're going and for what happens and what the implications of their work may be when they get there.

This is a project by Douglas Gordon from a show that I made a few years ago, in 1993-4, but it seemed interesting when I was looking through slides this week: I thought, 'Ah, it connects.' It was, after all, made in a disused flour mill. The show was called 'Walter Benjamin's Briefcase' and it was about a kind of hunt for an elusive object. This was in Porto in Portugal and when Douglas came to the space, he said, 'You know what I'd like to do? I'd like to take the fifth floor of this building out. Where it used to be, I'll put a tightrope and I'd like a guy to walk along the tightrope for the next two months.' Sure! So as the curator, I had to figure a few things out. First of all, you have to go to a structural engineer and see what they say about whether you can remove a floor without the building falling down. The first engineer said, 'no problem', but I was a bit nervous, so I got a second engineer in who said, 'oh no, you can't do that.' But with a third opinion, two out of three had said it was OK, so we removed the floorboards one by one, numbering them so they could go back later. Then we had to figure out the problem of where to find a tightrope walker in the middle of Portugal. Well, the answer is that you have to go to a circus school. We went to circus school in Lisbon and worked with a group of young circus artistes, and this becomes the heart of what an art practice might be today. I witnessed there, with the artist, a negotiation that was taking place in the name of art, where he spoke of his project, not in terms of a performance, but in terms of providing a space where they might be, and be themselves.

So the performers were saying, 'Well, you know, we can walk the tightrope whilst juggling,' and 'we can walk the tightrope whilst we do things with flames,' and Douglas said, 'No – just live up there and be yourself.' It became a very famous exhibition in Portugal, to the extent that the Prime Minister of Portugal's office called up one day and said, 'When does the guy walk on the tightrope?' And I get a message saying, 'The Prime Minister wants to come and see the guy walking the tightrope but we don't know when he walks and when he doesn't.' I said, 'Look, I don't know either!' That's the level of freedom that the artist gave the people who participated in his work. That's the level of freedom that one can try to give an artist when they're participating in an exhibition, because with that freedom you get unanticipated conjunctions, things that you hadn't thought of. You get relationships that take place that are, perhaps, outside of your realm of experience. And one method that I've been looking at to do this has been a series of exhibitions called 'Browser'.

I was commissioned to handle a triennial, quadrennial (I don't know what you would call it) that was taking place in Vancouver and was intended to represent the new generation of Canadian Art. The exhibition had a very long-standing tradition there and people were very fond of it. But of the hundreds of artists that I met and the studios I went to, no-one could ever remember any of the work that was in the shows – they just thought that the show was a nice idea. So I spent six months rummaging around trying to figure out a formula and I decided, you know what, why don't we make this the most inclusive show there could possibly be? If you perceive that you are an artist, that's it – you're in. You can be in this show and we will build an archive that can be animated, that contains real works of art and you, the audience, can be a curator, a participant in that work. What happens is that you come into the exhibition, you go down to the computer and the database is either on-line or on a CD-ROM. Let's say you're interested in landscape: you put in the word 'landscape' and there's about six works on landscape. You call up those works and you then can handle them.

This slide is the Vancouver installation. You can sit down at these desks and play with the work, or whatever, so you enter into a relationship with it. One of the things with a museum is that very often you're quite distant from the work. I'm very interested in exhibitions where you animate it in one form or another, either by walking through it or by participating in some form.

And you start to produce all sorts of unanticipated conjunctions.

Someone came down from the Brian Society in Seattle: it's a society the only qualification for membership of which is that your name has to be Brian. They came down and of course did a search on the 'Brians' that were in the show and they made a little 'mini-show' based on 'Brian-hood'! So there are many different ways of contributing to this, but the key thing for me is that you start to build up relationships between, if you like, very established, internationally visible artists, and those artists whose stories are just as interesting but who never are given a voice.

I became aware of this because one of the quirks of the Canadian funding system is that if you're doing a big-scale show like this, you have to have an open submission procedure. One day I got a video from someone and I thought it was a performance but it wasn't, it was very much 'from the heart'. This woman was dressed in a kind of artist's smock that painters are supposed to wear, with the beret and paint palette, etc., and she was talking as she was painting a very horrible blue painting. Had I just looked at the painting I wouldn't have cared, but her story was so interesting. She was using art in a way that I hadn't used art before – I hadn't thought art could work in that way. She was using it proactively, it was working for her; it did something. Not just as therapy but it actually occupied an important part in her world. How do we make a show which incorporates that? It's ironic that we've got a slide here of an artist whose contribution in her box was a leaflet which gave you art therapy – if you were freaked out by all this art you could call her up and she would try to resolve it.

Just before Tate Modern opened we did another manifestation of 'Browser' with the Tate to try to ask the question – and it's a very interesting question in relation to BALTIC, of course – which is, 'what constitutes the community for whom this building is being built? Who is it for? Is it for a kind of international circuit of artists/curators/tourists, or is there an obligation to the local that could be addressed in some way?' When we scripted the call for submissions, we tried to encourage, not just Londoners, but South Londoners, locals, to see if there was even a tenuous notion – and I hesitate to use the word but I will – of community. And it worked.

The point about a 'Browser' project like this is that you can have five hundred artists in the show. We're developing new 'Browsers' where we're looking at maybe a thousand artists being in the show and your version of 'Browser' and my version of 'Browser' are completely different, because I take a different journey through it. There was a reviewer who came to the Canadian version and she, very responsibly, wanted to see all the work. After three days of being in there for eight hours she still hadn't seen all the work, so she realised that it was bigger than all of us. That's what I like. And I like the fact that it's bigger than me as a curator.

You know, you're put in a position of trust and a position of power. People say, 'We're going to employ you because you've got some taste, or you've got some ethical position, or because you know how to organise the furniture.' It's got to be more than that. And it seemed to me that one of the issues was a) to be honest about who I am and when I talk about how I come to decisions, it's as much about my identity, but b) to relinquish some of the responsibility to allow other things to take place. It seems to me that starts to produce relationships that perhaps had not been anticipated before. And you start to have conversations in this space. I mean, the amazing thing when you go into one of these projects is that people start to become almost territorial about it for themselves. They start to say, 'Oh yes, I've seen that box and if you're interested in that box, then you should see that one.' So what we started to do was to give people curatorial space; invite people to curate shows within the space to try to make a way for people to animate this material. We train up twenty or thirty people to be the archivists, who also know the material really well. They engage with the artists when they submit the material, so there's a dialogue. The artists can describe their work; they can put a sound bite into the on-line database, or whatever. So there's a way of humanising the potentially inhuman nature of an archive, because this archive is constantly being animated.

This slide shows Antony Gormley's smallest sculpture, *Baby*. I believe the largest one is down the road! There's an irony that I hadn't thought of.

Really it's about privileging the viewer and the artist so that they can actually develop a space and so that their work can develop beyond itself. It's one thing to be an artist working in the studio, but it's a whole new set of relations when that work goes on its travels. It's unpredictable and it can go wrong, but sometimes it can really go right and there's something that's potentially very useful about that.

I've talked for fifteen minutes. I've done my bit. We'll get back to that later on.
Thank you.

(Audience applause)

My name is Sacha Craddock and what I'm going to do is to try and be really honest – as honest as I can be about how I'm doing what I'm doing now, but also maybe find out what it actually is. It's sometimes a bit hard for people to know what I do – if they're at all interested – but I do so many different kinds of things, and I think I might try and explain why that is. It's a kind of political decision on my part that requires a bit of background, which I'll speed through as quickly as I can.

Seventies – politics; end of the seventies – Thatcher got in. I thought, 'Oh no, there'll be no art school left, I'd better go to art school.' I felt guilty about it. I had a very naive political approach to this, thinking, 'It's bad to make art when I should be doing housing work or something.' I'd done a lot of trade union and legal work, had been a shop steward and then branch secretary for NUPE, had worked on some serious and notorious legal cases and been generally involved in all the things that one should have been involved with in the seventies. So I applied to art school – and this is, in a way, from a position of high sophistication. I went to St. Martin's and did a Foundation course, still not admitting to myself that I thought I could really be an artist.

One of my truisms that I'm going to come up with in the next quarter of an hour is the fact that you do much better doing the things you don't intend to do. I've fallen on everything in a very sideways way. If I'd set out to become a critic and do well at that, I'd never have got here, because I still feel guilty about painting. And I felt guilty when I was painting about not doing political work – get the picture? That's important for all of you, when you're thinking in a very fixed way that somehow you have to be incredibly directed in terms of what you're doing with your own work, with notions of accountability. Do not imagine that you can be that direct and you cannot be when you talk about responsibility – one is not actually completely responsible, especially with art which works in such a complex way.

When I got to St. Martin's I found a somewhat unworldly air. I found people unbelievably naive – and that was the tutors! I couldn't believe it. I suppose, though, any initial contact with a totally different context would be baffling. I found so much to learn but also so much that was small time, naive and deeply local in attitude. They said things like – and this is a political discussion – 'The Pope's a nice guy, isn't he?' And I thought, 'What have I come to?' That's the tutors after about eight pints: 'Nobody's looking at my work, but still, the Pope's a nice guy'– all this rubbish. If you come up through a discipline, and that is the only world you know, your concerns are really only the very nearest, your enemies also the very closest, to you. In politics, much more hatred was reserved for the leader of an obscure breakaway tendency than for obvious villains like Franco, who was still just about alive then.

My point is this: that if you divide out art practice from a kind of reality, you're in trouble. But they still thought you could. I remember sitting in a kitchen with a boyfriend and someone else and they were getting incredibly emotional about one particular kind of abstraction as opposed to another. Tutors used to argue the very smallest shift. 'Are you for us or against us?' they would say or imply, but real anger was reserved, especially at St. Martin's with its fine history, for John Latham, who ate a page of writing by Clement Greenberg. I'm thinking, 'I don't believe it. I think they're missing the point.' The art school is already nearly closing down, and they are going on like this! I mean, who cares? I have no moralism about art; I think people are totally over-moralistic.

I kept on seeing a gap there and I realised that the very basic principle of freedom was being undermined before my eyes – and that was the beginning of the eighties; we had no idea of what was to come. The same short-sightedness led later to an open-armed, apolitical acceptance of the notion of academic research, a desire to level peg with totally unrelated disciplines in a desperate attempt to be normal, real, and perhaps, anything other than an artist. The very difference of art, its lack of immediate effect or cause for instance, was being denied in a dangerous rush for parity.

So I did my painting and to tell you the truth, I did lyrical painting because I wasn't going to get involved in a moral, supposedly political, art campaign which didn't seem to follow. I couldn't see how it would work. I couldn't see that you could make work that would directly express some notion of the world. I heard, early on, the story of Georg Baselitz who, when starting out as a painter, wanted to make important paintings so painted important people: Beethoven, Marx, and so on, a complete folly. This direct and forced relation to subject was obviously not the answer. And so I did these giant lyrical things. I wasn't saying this was the answer either – they were just really good paintings, to put it mildly! But I didn't have the confidence to say, 'This is what I want to say.' Because another thing about making work is that it can't always be expressed verbally and this is one of my points.

In the meantime, I started doing a lot of speaking. I sat on boards, panels and so on. The first public speech was at the Whitechapel Art Gallery, somehow with Julian Schnabel. I always have been, and still am, quite happy to talk about anything. I found that there was my mother saying, 'Darling, how could you possibly talk about this ghastly stuff?' which I could and would, because I was immediately not deciding on a hierarchy of genre and I realised there was something more important going on that I needed to be involved in. This (discussion) is about curators, however, and I never really understood what curating was about until, perhaps, now. I used to imagine the word was over used: instead of saying you are organising an exhibition it is said that you are 'curating'.

Perhaps my initial attitudes to any encouragement to organise or curate shows was pretty basic, a continuation of my sideways attitude to life. I really didn't want to do it because if I could not make my own work then why would I want show anybody else's? This comes out of a particular direction and education. Instead of reading art history and understanding the work through the writing of essays, I come from a practical, practicing source. I came to writing through making work and there is still as much interest in the process as the result. They are very much the same thing. This is also about avoiding simple self-definition, the terrible pressure to say what particular gang or position you stand for. The very beginning of list making is hell, and makes an unnatural state out of art. The construction of a hierarchy can take art away from its own effect and context and reduce it to a mere shift in style.

I probably used to think that all the curator did was order the packing cases – but that's all changed now as in yet another non-deliberate move, I am part of a group of four who decide what happens in the new Bloomberg Space. The work at Bloomberg seems perfect, however. Working with three other people with a fantastic, frighteningly free brief, we discuss and argue, avoiding extreme personalisation.

Another thing I want to point out to you is this: when you first go to art school you know what you're not before you know what you are. And this is actually what's ruled my whole life. In other words, you define your art practice. A lot of the work you make is, in a way, reacting to other work. We are made by the negative space – negative/positive – in between other art.

Everybody pretends what they're doing now is to do with the world outside, but it's not – it's to do with other art on the whole. Very much of what one's involved in is a kind of question of definition. That's why, when I was asked to do this by Susan, I was thrilled. I think I eventually read one of the books and looked at the back and I said, 'Oh, it's about curating.' I suddenly read 'curating' and thought, 'I don't do that anyway!' What I do is choose things, I select things and I do it for very strong principles. Some people think I'm an expert on performance art, because I've written about that. Some people think, 'She's really good on the object,' which is what I'm into. I think the most radical thing you can do these days is to actually make something exist instead of making it disappear, I really do! The bigger the better! People didn't understand that when I was judging the Turner Prize two years ago – they were shocked!

I write on a tremendous range of things. Prunella Clough's a brilliant painter – I wrote about her and I really, really adore her work. Some people say, 'You really understand about painting.' Well, I understand about the need for people to be engaged in the process of making work through time, and defending that. And also defending the fact that the ultimate image, as it's called, is not going to lead one in terms of whether one's able to show it or not. In other words, what I see myself as doing is fighting, strangely, a liberal rearguard action, because although boring in politics, liberalism is dead essential when it comes to art.

I find it incredibly important to chair 'New Contemporaries'. It's incredibly important to be involved every year in the actual process of selection. I think that often, when people are selectors, what they do is to project onto the work the desire for it to succeed in its own terms. But what they should be doing is actually choosing from within the context of something that already exists, which I think is a really good defense. I've been with two selectors – once, unfortunately, when my father was dying and consequently I couldn't get in there and boss them about – that were saying, 'Oh, how ridiculous', about everything. In other words, you have to go with things at the level at which they exist. A lot of the work is really fantastic and the people who select have, on the whole, been amazing, so we produce a really considerable show. But I don't think it's curated; I think it's just about selecting.

In 1999 I was on the panel for The Turner Prize. Perhaps I should have been full of some strong fury about that, but I thought, 'OK, I'll do it.' And you know how I did that? I prepared every argument against people. You need to. Nobody questions enough, on the whole. Someone says, 'Oh, he/she is a very good person', you say 'why?' and they go, 'well, I mean, you know, she's shown ...' 'Tell me why.' So then I say why I don't think so and they go, 'My God, you're so prepared – you've worked hard.' It's not about being defensive and negative, but you actually have to be very strong.

I've just written a long essay in a book about a long and complicated work by Jochen Gerz – a well known and highly regarded German artist who lives in Paris. *Les Mots de Paris*, made throughout almost the whole of 2000 in Paris, is a little embarrassing to talk about – basically homeless people begged for money in the name of art. The press went mad and Gerz asked me, as an outsider, to write an unorthodox, open, questioning piece. I'm also helping set up The Brighton Photography Biennale (2003). I do a tremendous amount of teaching and think that teaching is brilliant – I enjoy it. Some people used to say to me, 'You don't have to do that any more.' Well I do, for money, but also it's important to me. I'm also writing lots of essays, mainly about painters, so this non-specialisation I mentioned has won out in the end.

I'm very worried about a certain tendency where we are obsessed with the notion of accountability in art. For instance, 'science and art', 'something and art' – the idea that it's all right as long as it's about something. Well, actually I reckon it's quite important to deal with what's there; to encourage what is possible and not, in a way, to find one's self in a situation like the Tate, where work is hung thematically and where you're also engaged in the notion of the account of the work. Or with students, you're looking at some picture and it's about immigration or something and you're saying, 'I'm sorry – can we now just all look at this? Now you be quiet, please. We'll look at this and see what it says and work back from the work itself.'

Another thing I just want to warn people about is when you sit chairing or judging something, like I've just judged a Jerwood Painting Prize, some of the people I was judging with kept on waiting for this art to do something for them: 'Oh, it just doesn't move me.' I was saying, 'It never will. It's not that brilliant!' No art does – it's about what one knows, being with it, spending time. The whole thing is this idea of waiting and in a way, there is a slight problem with the extreme increase of coverage in the press, which is personalised: people want the sensational, they want to think it's different, it breaks down barriers. I really think that what we do lose is the very basic principle of freedom to make, to support and to show art, when the infrastructure isn't there, in pursuit of something that is apparently extraordinary and exciting. I mean, artists talk about taking over whole cities or working in local authorities because it makes them feel more grown up, like not really artists. There is a kind of problem there. So I just thought I'd pose a few questions.

(Audience applause)

SACHA CRADDOCK (TO ANDREW RENTON):

I saw your project in the Tate and I would just like to say
– I think we're meant to be contentious with one another
– that I felt that project did exactly the opposite to what
was intended. It was totally not about showing people's
work. You couldn't see the work because it was in
boxes. Politically, it felt at the time – and it's not your
fault because it's a good idea, in a way – that the Tate
was using that as a sop to people in the local
community. We have a problem with people who make
work in this country because we feel guilty about it –
everyone feels guilty about art, and then to put it away in
boxes and to have to have gloves on to look at it...

ANDREW RENTON:

I think you're absolutely right. I feel very strongly about
this project that it must work within the framework of the
institution and with the Tate project, the institution found
it quite hard to figure out what it was meant to do. One
of the points of principle for me is that no artist's name
is promoted ahead of another. The most important thing
is that there's got to be that equality. In Vancouver, for
example, there are six ultra-famous artists there who do
all the travelling around the world, and then there are a
whole bunch of other people who don't get any action.
What we discovered is that if you don't promote those
names, people start to use it in the way they want to use
it. So they don't go for famous names. It's amazing. They
don't rush in for the Antony Gormley, the Damien Hirst,
the Jeff Wall or whatever. They run in for the things that
they are passionate about.

SACHA CRADDOCK:

It's the same with subjects, like landscape. I mean, it's not to do with the way something exists physically in the world, which is what art's about. You either go for a 'Brian' or a 'landscape'.

ANDREW RENTON:

Yes. Or you could search for women or for photographs.

SACHA CRADDOCK:

Pornography would be more useful, wouldn't it?

ANDREW RENTON:

That was the other interesting thing, because we were very alert to something like that. The amazing thing is that people chose not to abuse it. What happens if someone put something into the collection that is kind of problematic? The thing is, it's got this self-regulating quality. The main thing to say in response to you is that it changes from place to place. We're looking, for example, at doing it in other countries. Lots of other countries have invited us to do things and one that I'm playing with is the idea of doing an Israeli/Palestinian 'Browser', for example, where you construct a situation in which things are put together that would never normally get put together...

SACHA CRADDOCK:

But you don't see them together. It's just the notion.

ANDREW RENTON:

But you do. I mean, you don't see them together here but you see them in a temporary way. You can configure it in another way where you can actually have displays, which we did have, that were on for three or four days at a time and then were changed and taken down. The Tate space didn't really allow for that and that was one of the frustrations.

SACHA CRADDOCK:

Also there's no freedom in the notion of scale, you know. Everything's reduced from this to that and that's a real problem.

JOHN MILNER:

That's true, but you were talking about the difficulties, and pleasures, actually, of being a selector. Andrew, having a fixed format is about not selecting, in a way, but (to Sacha) you're accusing him of not allowing enough freedom in there. There seems to be something a bit contradictory in that.

SACHA CRADDOCK:

There's no contradiction. It's just that it's not art in there – it's little thingys in boxes and they're all hidden. It does have a kind of physical presence as a whole, but otherwise it's a container thing. I'm not being facetious, but I find it difficult. The most important thing would be to just organise shows of more work.

ANDREW RENTON:

Yes, but that was the point. That was what we were trying to deal with. I have curated those big biennial shows. I was asked to submit a proposal for 'Manifesta', this new European biennial. I wrote half a page and I faxed it off on a Friday afternoon saying, 'It's the worst idea in the world; we don't need any more biennials.' Big shows are boring, they're hard on the feet – I have arthritis, I can't walk through all of that stuff. Guess what? A week later they gave me the job!

JOHN MILNER:

And you took it?

ANDREW RENTON:

I took it! But what I tried to do, with my four colleagues, was to divert the funds and set up a foundation that funded art projects throughout a two-year period. That was a no-no: you can't get funds unless you're doing a blockbuster. So then we said, 'What if we divide it into a series of projects so that you don't feel as if you have to see the whole thing, but instead you can go to one place and see one show?' That was a compromise, but frankly, I sold out, trust me! If you're trying to voice a problem with that kind of project, do you back out on ideological grounds, or do you stay in and have a voice? I chose to stay in.

SACHA CRADDOCK:

Well, you stay in and just show some art – that's fine.

ANDREW RENTON:

Yes, but the problem with the original point is that when you get to a certain stage, you develop this kind of rhetorical blindness where you can't see the wood for the trees – then you've got a problem. That's not democracy. Democracy is when things are made visible by one means or another. And it occurred to me that the format that produced 'Browser' was not democratic; it didn't enrich by providing relationships. My solution is by no means a perfect one – it's flawed, deeply flawed, but it was an extreme strategy to try to get something going. I know it doesn't always work but I also know that it produces another effect, which is actually quite human and interactive.

JOHN MILNER:

And quite accessible to people.

ANDREW RENTON:

I think so.

JOHN MILNER:

Sacha, you are involved in quite a few ventures that deal
with young artists. This is a vital link that very few people
talk about. The question, which is obviously a live issue
in a place like this, the Slade or St. Martin's, is how does
the young artist connect with opportunities to display
their work? Also, if you're dealing with prizes, this is
obviously going to exclude people: most people don't
get them.

SACHA CRADDOCK:

There is a problem with prizes because they create the
false idea that the minute you focus on say, just four
people, then that becomes, in a way, the whole world.
Even worse than that are books about who's important
and who isn't – I don't know how any state institution
can support this kind of business. But there's the
extraordinary idea that there is this fixed notion of art and
it is a particular line and a particular area. I think much
more abstract discussion should be encouraged around
it. Now, on the issue of young people not getting enough
opportunities: I get a bit bored with young people
getting so many opportunities! Sorry, I'm just stirring and
winding you up. I came up to Newcastle two years ago
and I saw the exhibition 'VANE' and I enjoyed that. I liked
that aspect of taking over a place and doing it yourself.
Unfortunately there wasn't enough money and some of
the places were a bit musty, but it was good in some
respects. What happened in art schools in the mid-
eighties was that there were people coming in to talk

about professional life after art school – professional this, that and the other.

There are things you can do: there's a lot of self-help, there's a lot of showing your own work and so on, and something like 'New Contemporaries' is incredibly important. But these are much bigger questions and there are certain other sorts of work that aren't shown, or institutions are not able to show people at a certain stage of their career. You know, when you think about a lot of very good abstract painting in this country, people are so isolated in relation to that, they end up painting the same thing over and over. It becomes so bad because it's not allowed to breathe. Whereas if you go to IVAM in Valencia, for example, there'll be the younger stuff and then there'll be someone from another generation. It might not be the most gripping work, but it gets seen and discussed. So the infrastructure's a bit hopeless here. We're obsessed with youth and lifestyle, groovy yBa-type stuff, which is rubbish and, thank God, completely out of date now. You have to be quite good at making art as well – it helps! I don't look at absolute rubbish and say, 'Well done'. But I think what matters is that maybe people don't get enough teaching; maybe it's to do with money being spent in another way.

JOHN MILNER (TO ANDREW RENTON):

You've put the 'Browser' show on in different cities and had different responses. Is this an inevitable part of the art world these days, where there are these big international exhibitions and reputations are also international?

ANDREW RENTON:

What's inevitable is the international exhibitions. What's not inevitable and what's completely ignored are the local circumstances, which should relate to where you get to see the art. It's incredibly important if you're making an exhibition that you know where it is that you're making it. Otherwise you've got this kind of 'rock star' scenario where someone comes in and says, 'Good evening, Gateshead,' when in fact they're in Stockholm!

SACHA CRADDOCK:

What do you mean? Do you mean people that make work should be sensitive to the place they're making work in? I think they overdid that: that whole history of place, everyone being totally fetishistic about it being a closed-down factory, or whatever.

JOHN MILNER:

No one's like that around here!

ANDREW RENTON:

I'm kind of interested in two things. I'm interested in those spaces, but I'm also interested in the question of what on earth we make exhibitions for, unless there is a resonance that happens afterwards. What is the point of just doing a show? It seems to me that if you're making a show in a particular place, what would be really useful – bearing in mind exhibitions are expensive things to put on – would be to make them in a place where the consequence of your making that project allows other things to happen. For example, with the Douglas Gordon project, we spent a lot of money putting that building together. We worked with huge local teams, including all the local art schools. Now, the direct consequences of that exhibition are a) there is an infrastructure that puts on exhibitions because we set it up; b) there's a building that puts on exhibitions and c) there's actually a fantastic art scene in Porto now and there wasn't five or six years ago. I'm not saying it was just because of our show – it was a collective effort that used an exhibition as a premise for all sorts of other relationships. I'm also thinking about BALTIC and what that ought to be doing here. It's not just about whether or not you get a gig in there; it's about the implications of all the spin-offs that come with that. The most interesting thing is that if you don't get a gig in there you can set up all sorts of alternatives so that I have to come here every two months to catch up.

JOHN MILNER:

Sacha, you were talking about political awareness earlier on. You said that you didn't want the art to be paying too obvious lip service to that: that you couldn't think of a way yourself of connecting what you were doing in the studio with something you were doing outside.

SACHA CRADDOCK:

Well, I'm very perverse and I also feel that there's a problem here in terms of the way an artist actually speaks, what an artist says, and the fact that it's very hard for people, especially when they're starting out, to learn that what they can do is, in a way, very limited. Therefore, I kind of understood immediately that one couldn't illustrate one's understanding of the world but, through doing a tremendous number of different things, one does. I think everyone here knows that they make work, or they study work, but they do many other, different things as well, and I think that's what brings together an understanding. It isn't necessarily reflected in the work.

JOHN MILNER:

But do you share Andrew's view that you can change a whole environment, in all sorts of ways?

SACHA CRADDOCK:

We were talking on the train up about the Liverpool
Biennial, about certain cities and so on. Actually, I think
this city has got a fantastic history with art. I remember
coming up for 'A New Necessity' (First Tyne International
Exhibition of Contemporary Art, 1990) and then coming
up for something else, then less and then more: it comes
and goes and it depends on funding.

JOHN MILNER:

Both speakers were talking about ways of creating
'opportunities' – that's not quite the word, but involving
artists who might not necessarily have well-established
reputations. There may be some such people in the
room with us, who knows? We have quite a lot of art
students here: do you have feelings about Sacha's
statement that, for example, you can go too far in
preparing students for professional life after art school?
We have little sessions about life after art school here –
they've just been dismissed. It's an important thing to
bridge with the professional world of the artist, or do you
think we should be more radical and do something
different?

SACHA CRADDOCK:

Of course it's all well and good to do that. What I'm
talking about is that I've often found in art schools now
that any real criticism of work has been replaced by
some notion of 'career' in a very obvious way. So, with
'New Contemporaries' for instance, I organised a day in
which the artists in the exhibition came together to have
a really heavy, critical time about one another's work.
That's what might be missing at times. There are even
places, like the Royal College, that bring in dealers to
teach. What does that mean to you? Does it mean that
you think everyone is going to get a leg-up and a bit of

help with their dreadful little painting, and someone's come around and tipped the wink that they don't have to do any more, so they give up working? The interaction has to be a bit more subtle than that. Do you know what I'm saying? No? Well, maybe you don't have lots of dealers here.

QUESTION (TO ANDREW RENTON):

Can I ask you a question about the status of the artist? What I find most interesting about the way you describe the 'Browser' project is your creativity. I feel I'm looking at you as an artist and that aspect of you interests me. But I wondered whether you're somehow diminishing the artists to the context of the box and if so, how you feel about that?

ANDREW RENTON:

I think you've asked two questions and I'll answer the second one first and then get to the other one, which I think might open something else up in terms of what curatorial practice might be.

The box problem. I'll be honest with you: when we first did this thing in Vancouver, once a month I would have an open forum with anyone who wanted to talk about how this project was developing. After six months I said, 'Look, I really want to make this inclusive and we've come up with this formula and this is how it is.' And I'd describe the process of putting things in the boxes. The next day it was front-page news in the newspaper that I had somehow tyrannised the art community. The headline was, 'Curator wants to put artists in a box.' I'd like to think of it in the opposite terms, because the main thing I wanted to do was to get the artists out of the box. For sure, it's not adequate. It doesn't do the whole job, but it does do something that other exhibitions don't, and it does provide relationships that others don't. I am troubled by the scale and the practicality of it. It's a challenge, like working within any other space.

This problem leads to the first half of your question, which is the real curatorial trouble spot: what role does the curator have as a creative person within the exhibition-making process? I am troubled by that because I'm not an artist. My background is distinctly non-visual and yet I feel I'm obsessed with trying to make things visible. I've made projects where I'm very much part of the project and it's often emerged from a dialogue with artists; projects where my correspondence and my dialogue with artists is made visible. It comes from a point which I feel quite strongly about, which is that when I was a kid going round museums, I never quite knew who was doing the manipulating. I never quite knew how it worked or who made those decisions, because the curator was invisible. It seemed to me that there might be an ethical obligation for the curator to be visible: for him or her to come clean as to their agenda, as to who they are, and I've even made exhibitions where an almost autobiographical element has come out. I remember giving a lecture in Toronto about my work and as I walked into the lecture hall I saw a poster for it and my name was superimposed on a Union Jack flag! My grandparents came to this country from Syria, my great-grandparents came from Russia – they all came because they were dispossessed. The idea that the Union Jack is something with which I am associated seemed extraordinarily problematic. So the next project along, I think, 'I've got to tell people what my agenda is in order to be honest about where the manipulations are taking place.' I think manipulations do take place on the part of the curator and I think that sometimes we do step inside the project a little too much.

QUESTION:

Do you think curating as an activity is distinct from being an artist?

ANDREW RENTON:

It's blurred. I've made a decision, for example, that I don't make artworks but I collaborate with artists on a regular basis in terms of their work. The hardest thing is to know when to close your mouth. The worst thing you can say is, 'You know what you ought to do...' I think that's the worst thing you could do as a curator, and I think I've learnt that. What I can do though is talk through all sorts of contexts on a very personal level. There's a kind of contradiction in there because on the one hand I'm saying I want to put myself in the frame, but on the other hand, I'm doggedly resisting the idea of the practice of making art. Today I don't know whether there is a viable distinction between the artist and the curator. I've been in shows curated by artists, and that's very interesting. I think there's enough fluidity that there is a range of models available. But I do feel quite strongly that you have to be up-front about who you are and if that implies a kind of over-presenting of yourself, then I apologise for that because I definitely try not to do that either. So I've answered your question by not answering it!

JOHN MILNER:

The way you were talking, Sacha, it seemed to me that you felt very strongly that one shouldn't talk about the work all the time.

SACHA CRADDOCK:

No, I think people should talk about the work – not what people *think* it's saying. I think people have lost confidence in their ability to see and know that what they see is actually telling them something. I think that students and the public are always being talked to, in a way, and actually it's quite important to start with the artwork and work back from it. It sounds terribly simple but it really is true. There's a whole air of guilt about making art, a whole line of justification, whereas in fact it's fine, it doesn't matter. I'm so against that kind of moralism. I watched something on television once where there was a bit of cynicism about the Independent Group. I mean, who cares? This work is perfectly all right on its own terms and it's a matter of understanding history and the politics surrounding it – actually understanding work more. A good curator, maybe in a grand institution as opposed to something more adventurous, will help you see and think better. We don't have enough confidence in visual language still and we surround it with talk, but usually it's just about looking, not about a construction that runs parallel to it.

JOHN MILNER:

If you're working on 'New Contemporaries', for example, to what extent does the idea of coherence in the show take over, or do you consider each of the submitted works independently?

SACHA CRADDOCK:

It has to be considered independently and separately, although in the end there is discussion and patterns do emerge. When Susan was selecting, certain patterns did emerge which were very much of the time and you could look back afterwards and see that things had something in common. There are certain feelings at certain times around work that make it fascinating. For instance, the fact that a few years ago nobody could deal with anything that had any physicality and yet now there's people like Mike Nelson or Keith Tyson who are somehow being understood much later on. The dislike of the existence of almost anything has meant that sculptural practice or object-ness has been a very problematic thing.

Let me just simplify things. Eighties: everything was so difficult, but at least you could say 'that's real' (banging table), with the physical object. Nineties: we'd all gone through that easy-peasy postmodern stuff, saying, 'but of course it wasn't real'. Then we got on to imagery – we were obsessed with imagery – and now there's suddenly a sense that actually, something can exist and we don't have to feel totally guilty about something that takes up a lot of space or that you don't turn off at night.

ANDREW RENTON:

That was very visible in the last 'New Contemporaries', which was incredibly exuberant, incredibly physical.

SACHA CRADDOCK:

And a lot of that was turned off at night! There were some very good videos, weren't there?

ANDREW RENTON:

But it actually felt like a show to me. I think that at its best, a framework like 'New Contemporaries' can show you things that nothing else can and I loved that show precisely because it felt like a show.

QUESTION:

I just wanted to open up some issues around some of the things that people have been discussing: putting large groups of artists together in boxes, young artists versus the rest, opportunities and just what it is exhibitions are about. I wanted to go back to an experience that I had with Sacha selecting 'New Contemporaries'. One thing that I think she's been very reticent about is how much energy and courage it takes to sustain that exhibition to make sure it happens every year. This is an enormous achievement, so clearly there's belief there. The interesting experience that I wanted raise was what it was like to see, alongside the work that was selected for the first Liverpool Biennial (1999) – and this is something that really hasn't been talked about – these young artists whose show is better than the Biennial. What does that mean? It wasn't better in the sense of being trendy or fashionable. In fact, Keith Tyson, Carolyn Christov-Bakargiev and I selected what I think was probably a deeply unfashionable show, but it was just better. And it was embarrassing to have people from Tate, for example, say, 'Oh, this is a really nice room! This is the best room!' And we were going, 'Yes, they're still at art school.' In a way, the truth is that not all those people will have the opportunity to make it to the next Liverpool Biennial. And then you come to much more profound questions, I think, about what art represents in our society, what function it has and why it is we practise art rather than other forms of creativity. What is at the root of denigrating so much talent, which is actually the experience of most artists in this country, because although there is a tremendous amount of hype around art, there's hardly any opportunity for anybody? Those questions came out in both of your talks and really, if we're going to talk about curating, selecting, putting exhibitions together, we have to see that we're still molecules in all of this, rather than decision makers. We're not exactly sure what we're doing. Anyway, I just wanted to see if anyone in the audience could respond to any of that because it is very, very tricky.

QUESTION:

I think that because grants have been taken away from students, these people have to pay more money just to get to art college, therefore maybe more opportunities are being taken away than have actually been provided. But I quite agree that more opportunities should be made further along in an artist's career.

SACHA CRADDOCK:

I agree and I think there's a complete contradiction there. Years ago, with 'New Contemporaries', we talked about whether there should be a prize and I said that instead of a prize, there should be more grants for teaching – quite simple. We've gone through a strange time, from when I was writing for *The Guardian*, when nobody wrote about anything contemporary, to it being non-stop, but more 'lifestyley'. We've gone through a real shift of attention, but what is not really being dealt with is an open approach to art – the fact that there is a lot of it and it's really good to see and people are really quite capable of judging for themselves. It would be great for people to not like stuff; to have the chance to think, 'It's not good'; to actually look at some rather average paintings and think, 'OK, fine' and to get the chance to be involved in discussion. The infrastructure's a bit hopeless now and so many galleries in London have stopped showing work in that way. It's a problem.

ANDREW RENTON:

It is a problem. I look at my students and I don't quite know how they're going to figure it out, because the education system now works on the assumption that if you get yourself an education, then you can go out and get a job, earn a regular salary and therefore pay back your loan. Well, making art doesn't work like that. That doesn't make it less valid, but the consequence of that is you kind of retreat: you make less art which then produces a sort of loop. We're caught in a paradox because we all recognise that's a problem. On the other hand, I would argue that something like Tate Modern got built precisely because the environment existed in London as a consequence of a small group of artists who were very hot. Five million people a year go through that building, it's free, and there are possibilities there. So there's a trade-off and someone has to pay the price. Unfortunately it's probably at the education end and what Sacha was pointing towards is a role for the artist to play that is not linked exclusively to the market and to exhibiting, and that's the X-factor. There needs to be a place for the artist, and it's interesting that however high profile the lifestyle artist might be today, they don't actually have a place in society – they don't actually do anything in the world. I do think that there are possibilities for art to actually inhabit places that it doesn't currently, but we're caught in the loop and I perpetuate it because my job is to make exhibitions. I would love to find a way of dislocating that.

QUESTION:

I'd just like to join in on that. I actually think there is quite a lot of money around for the production of art: there are some very large-scale commissions and grants for research. But it seems to me that one of the problems about a lot of the money that is made available for the production of art is that it's often tied to a kind of commodification brief. When we do have funding for art it is already tied to the notion of the market and what we don't do is liberate that money somehow or renegotiate how that money is distributed. Just very, very simply say, 'Use this money to support the practice of art.' We used, at one time, to have grants for artists and studios. In a way, there was a real reaction against that kind of funding because it was abused or it wasn't accountable. But unless you allow work to be made, then the notion of openness within the practice of art – as an artist and not as an object-maker or a commodity provider – is totally stifled.

ANDREW RENTON:

Absolutely. I wonder how we get to that point, though? I mean, we've all filled out those forms and the nature of those forms is about, 'What are you going to produce with this?' It seems to me that the biggest luxury any of us could have as practitioners, either as curators or as artists, is to ask a question. The biggest problem that you have when you're filling in the form is that it's all end-related and the irony is that 'research' doesn't mean research any more: research means product.

JOHN MILNER:

You're given university grants to finish research and that rather confirms what you're saying. One more question, please and then we've got to stop.

QUESTION:

Andrew, I believe that you are curating, or being asked to curate, the M.F.A. interim show at the Slade and I actually find that quite interesting in relation to the critical remarks Sacha made earlier about professional practice. What do you hope to achieve by curating an interim MFA show? What attracted you to this?

ANDREW RENTON:

First of all, I feel that what I do as a curator is always linked to what I do within the art school. I feel very strongly about my obligations there, either as a teacher or as a participant within that framework, so I don't draw a distinction. I have a role at the Slade that has evolved through trying to figure out something that is missing in art schools, which is that standing-back process. Often, as an artist in an art school, you're inside your studio and there's physically not enough space to stand back from your work, and there's an extraordinary kind of interdependence between students that is never really analysed. In the rush to do degree shows, there's no finessing of that relationship, no addressing of what the relationship might be. So we looked at the idea of an interim show that had no obligations anywhere: it wasn't about being assessed.

JOHN MILNER:

It's a very tricky idea.

ANDREW RENTON:

Absolutely. But that was the deal that I wanted to strike: that it was not obligatory; it had to be self-determined, and it is part of my obsession that if you've made a commitment to going to art school, then you've made a commitment to being an artist. It's an exhibition – I don't care whether it's at the Slade or outside of the Slade. I care that it's a group of artists who will develop a relationship with each other in a situation that is additional to whatever the educational programme is there. I'm on the line with it because I know there's a lot of expectation in terms of producing something, but I feel quite strongly about it. I'm excited about it and I take it very seriously.

JOHN MILNER:

I'd like to ask Sacha to respond to this, because here, on the face of it, is a curator and a teacher in an art school setting up an opportunity for a really quite vigorous debate between the people working there as young artists.

SACHA CRADDOCK:

I think there's a real problem in art schools where people pretend they're not at art school. For instance, the curating course at the Royal College puts on exhibitions and they're playing grown-ups really. But then if you so much as criticise it, it's OK, they're students – it's kind of real but it's not real. It's within the institution so it's quite important to admit it's an institution. I think it's quite a good thing to do, but I think that if it's about self-determination, then you should be self-determined. At a certain point one has to stand back and let them do it – which is what I hope you're doing (To Andrew). So the idea of selecting work from within something which is self-determined is a bit odd, it's contradictory.

ANDREW RENTON:

I'm not selecting...

SACHA CRADDOCK:

OK. It's jolly good to give people the opportunity but it's also good that people don't have to do it, although of course they'll all be racing like mad to do it! But what I'm really interested in is that you said you're putting yourself on the line because a lot is expected. What is expected? What is expected from the institution – a finished exhibition, looking like any exhibition in the boring old world, or is it about students learning to be artists and dealing with working together and having a discussion? What do you think they want?

JOHN MILNER:

Oh, you really want the answer to that?

SACHA CRADDOCK:

I'm interested because there's always this expectation from within art schools, which is completely false.

JOHN MILNER:

Quite right – all sorts of invisible expectations.

SACHA CRADDOCK:

I just think that's an interesting thing and I also think.... Oh, let's go and have a drink!

JOHN MILNER

Quite right! Thank you.

(Audience applause)

THE PRODUCERS: CONTEMPORARY CURATORS IN CONVERSATION

6 FEBRUARY 2002, UNIVERSITY OF NEWCASTLE, DEPARTMENT OF FINE ART

JONATHAN WATKINS AND LAURA GODFREY-ISAACS IN CONVERSATION CHAIRED BY ANDREW BURTON

VICKI LEWIS:

Hello and welcome to this, the penultimate 'Producers' at this particular venue. As I am sure you are all aware, this series is focused on the role of the curator in initiating, commissioning and presenting contemporary art. It is organised by BALTIC Professor Susan Hiller and funded jointly by the University of Newcastle and BALTIC, with the proceedings published in the B.READ series of books. Our two distinguished curators tonight are Jonathan Watkins and Laura Godfrey-Isaacs.

Jonathan Watkins joined Ikon in Birmingham as director in 1999, following his appointment as artistic director of the 11th Sydney Biennale. Previously he worked for a number of years with major galleries in London: as curator of the Serpentine Gallery from 1995 to 1997 and director of Chisenhale Gallery from 1990 to 1995. As a guest curator, Jonathan Watkins has contributed to a number of projects, including 'Quotidiana' at Castello di Rivoli, Turin (1999 –2000), and 'Europarte', the Biennale di Venezia (1997). He was British Commissioner for 'Milano Europa 2000', Milan, and guest curator for 'Facts of Life', an exhibition of contemporary Japanese art at the Hayward Gallery, London (2001). He is also guest curator for the forthcoming 'Tate Triennale' at Tate Britain (spring 2003).

Laura Godfrey-Isaacs is an artist, curator and academic. She trained as a painter at the Slade School of Art and in New York on a Fulbright Fellowship. Key exhibitions have included 'Pink' at Tate Liverpool, 'Slime' at the Sue Williams Gallery, London, and 'Monstrous' at the Gallery at John Jones, London. In 1998 she ceased her practice as an artist and set up the arts organisation HOME, which is based inside her family house in Camberwell, London. HOME works collaboratively with a range of international artists who realise exhibitions, performances, events, talks and workshops from within the functioning spaces of her house.

Last, but not least, our chair for tonight, Andrew Burton, who is an artist and also the head of the Fine Art Department here at the University of Newcastle. So Andrew, over to you.

ANDREW BURTON:

Thank you very much. Well, the format we are going to follow tonight is exactly the same as we have done in the past. Each of our speakers is going to speak for fifteen or twenty minutes about their recent projects and where they might be going and then the discussion will be opened up to the floor. Jonathan is going to go first.

JONATHAN WATKINS:

Thank you. I am going to talk about recent and not so recent projects. Susan asked me if I would cast my mind back to the good old days when I was running Chisenhale, from 1990 to 1995, and then provide a summary of my curatorial activity since then to the present day. It's an interesting exercise for me, because I very rarely get the chance to concentrate on my work in this way, to divine or try to distil some sort of discernible development through my activity. Certainly there is a basic philosophy informing what I do, but also without question, my practice as a curator has changed, inevitably reflecting changes in contemporary art practice. Above all, perhaps, illustrated by the sequence of slides that I am about to show, there is an impulse to move out of dedicated art space.

At Chisenhale there was a certain fetishisation of the white cube-type space, which is something that I think I have lost along the way, perhaps: a certain preciousness, which corresponds to changing attitudes with respect to installation, as an art form, and the way artists deal with the site-specificity.

Considering all the art projects I've been involved with, the one that epitomises my current position is On Kawara's *Pure Consciousness*. Started in Sydney at the 1998 Biennale, this is an ongoing project that happens in kindergartens in cities all over the world. It consists of seven 'date paintings', embodying the artist's activity during seven consecutive days, and they are installed in rooms where children are just about to latch on to the business of reading. In this slide you can see counting books underneath the date paintings, so in effect, the children are in the process of learning to count with On

Kawara. I am interested in the fact that this artwork takes place beyond the walls of museums and galleries and, in fact, is virtually inaccessible to the art crowd. It is appealing to a completely non-specialist audience. I also like the way that it plays off its context and believe that the context is absolutely crucial, not only when it comes to deriving possible meanings from a work, but also to the identity of the work of art itself.

It is significant how the kindergarten is a room not unlike those depicted in earlier drawings by On Kawara, his almost Surrealist depictions of warehouse interiors and bathrooms, made during the fifties. His subsequent career carries on a fascination with the way art is installed in rooms. Kindergartens are inhabited by all sorts of things that can't be designed or controlled, including the way children often behave.

Going back, then, to the 'good old days'. The first show that I was involved with at Chisenhale – although not initiated by me – was Rachel Whiteread's *Ghost* (1990). It taught me a lot about the nature of installation. A plaster cast domestic room, a fossilisation of domestic space, it was foiled by a vast space beyond it – Chisenhale's shoebox-like space of 1,000 cubic metres. However, the density of this work is only one half of the story. The other half is the void, the emptiness on the other side, the eloquence and the power of that. Whiteread's installation counteracted notions of her work as a discrete object, but instead asserted its relation to the gallery interior.

Shortly afterwards I commissioned a work by Cornelia Parker, *Cold Dark Matter: An Exploded View*, exhibited at Chisenhale in 1991. It started with a garden shed, standing as a symbol for home and the idea of shelter, security. And then there was the explosion, followed by a reconstitution of the shed, or its constituent parts, into a solar system of distressed fragments of wood and other household objects, revolving around a domestic light bulb. It was about moving beyond spaces we think we know.

Another one of the strongest exhibitions at Chisenhale, arguably, was that of Absalon's *Cellules* in 1995. Again, there was the strong motif of the room, or a small space for living in, as with Whiteread and Parker. Absalon was designing these cells with the idea that they were actual-size prototypes for stopping-off places, for his own occupancy, as he moved around the world. There would be one in Paris, one in Zurich, one in Tokyo and so on. In fact, they were more like tombs as Absalon was dying of AIDS at the same time as he was developing this project. They proposed a paradoxical fusion of spaces for both art and life. Before the end, in 1993, he finished six prototypes in a very intense burst of activity, and we showed four.

In terms of the way I was thinking about space – exhibition space and inhabitable space generally – and with respect to the way my curatorial activity has developed since, the exhibition of work by Ann Veronica Janssens and Richard Venlet at Chisenhale in 1993 was perhaps most telling. The artists made minimal interventions within the gallery. You'll see in this slide, for example, a window high up on the right-hand side. Normally it is invisible, and it was a question of removing plasterboard to allow natural light into the gallery. There's a small dot (in the slide) – that's because Ann Veronica inserted a long brass pipe into the end wall. Through it you could see the derelict rooms of the next-door brewery that had recently gone bankrupt. It was like looking through a telescope onto a vignette of a different and disorganised world.

Both artists decided to remove the door between the office and the gallery so that the art space was continuous with our administrative space – and also the roller shutter between the reception area and the street – thus appropriating space for their exhibition that they hadn't designed. What struck me most was the possibility of blurring the line between the place for art and everything else. I mean, where exactly did the art start and stop? That was, for me, the very interesting question that this project raised.

Shortly after this I went to the Serpentine and there I was responsible primarily for the programme that ran up to the refurbishment of the gallery, and then I undertook a number of off-site projects during the time when the building was closed. The last exhibition in the 'old' Serpentine was an installation by Richard Wilson, for which he had more freedom than any artist previously had, in terms of the imposition made on the architectural fabric, due to the imminent construction work. Site huts, like those used by the contracted builders, were the point of departure for Richard. He sliced through them, and swapped sections of them with parts of the old Serpentine building. Circular sections, for example, of the corner of a wall and floor, or shelves from the bookshop, were inserted into the site huts, while bits of huts could be found around the gallery. The artist was testing the extremes of identity, between the work of art and its environment. When does one become the other thing? When does something become so grafted that it loses its identity, becomes less of a site hut and more of the Serpentine? This exhibition literally broke through the membrane that separated the gallery interior from the world beyond.

Richard Wilson was, to some extent, reiterating the proposition made by Fischli and Weiss in their exhibition at the Serpentine earlier in 1996. These two artists made the most of the glazed walls of the Serpentine – those wonderful windows that make the Serpentine a very special place. Left uncovered, if you are inside, they enable you to be aware equally of what's going on outside. This perfectly suited Fischli and Weiss who are always concerned to stress the continuity between art and non-art/life. This tendency was most evident perhaps in their polyurethane sculptures which resembled readymades, bits and pieces to do with gallery technical work: a breathing mask, for example, or a tube of silicone; a bucket or a cassette tape. Even the bits of basic material that looked like pieces of polystyrene blanks were sculpted and painted to look like that. Besides the witty game of double-take, which confused many visitors attending the private view ('had we finished installing the show?'), they exemplified a strong and optimistic assertion of art embedded in everyday life.

It was this exhibition, as well as the ongoing conversation that I had with the artists, that led to my proposition for the Biennale of Sydney (2000). I left the Serpentine in 1997 in order to start working on this big exhibition, involving about a hundred artists from all over the world. Fischli and Weiss were very important to me as I was starting to develop and articulate the idea. I had a number of discussions with them about what was ordinary: ideas of an 'everyday sublime', what was ordinarily extraordinary, extraordinarily ordinary or just ordinarily ordinary. I agonised over managing to strike a balance, how to get it right – also to avoid going down boring or sentimental roads into the everyday world. The title of the exhibition was 'Every Day', with emphasis on the everyday nature of things and also the idea of everyday coming and going, so that a lot of work in it – like On Kawara's *Pure Consciousness* – overtly embodied the passage of time. My desire to escape 'art space' manifested itself in a relatively large component of offsite projects which took place around six indoor venues.

This slide depicts a work by Danish artist Olafur Eliasson: a synthetic waterfall that was in the Botanic Gardens in Sydney, significantly placed between a manicured natural environment and the high-rise business district of Sydney. Here we see a work by Perry Roberts, a large billboard on the end of a maritime warehouse on Sydney Harbour. As you pulled away from it by boat, you could see how it was keyed into the basic gridded fabric of Sydney – like a colour chart, picking up not only on the basic structure of the modernist architecture, but also on predominant colours. It was a very site-specific piece of abstraction.

The work of Martin Creed in the Sydney Biennale had a similar rigour and unpretentiousness (*Work no. 200 – half the air in a given space*). It was his biggest balloon installation to date, with 165,000 balloons inflated in a three-storey Harbour Master's House with a viewing tower on an island in the middle of Sydney Harbour. It was an incredibly claustrophobic experience between the front door and the staircase, so that walking up the stairs, somewhere between the first and second floors, moving up out of the first layer of balloons, was like being in an aeroplane breaking through clouds.

This emphasis on sensory experience was developed further in 'Facts of Life': an exhibition of contemporary Japanese art that I curated recently for the Hayward Gallery (Oct – Dec 2001). Here, for example, is work by Yukio Fujimoto, an artist who has been around for some time but has not shown in this country before. These are his *Ear Pipes*: lengths of plastic pipe which visitors to the exhibition place over their ears in order to transform their experience of hearing ambient sound. Fujimoto is fascinated by the nature of human perception: the fact of life that you can't feel, hear or otherwise sense things beyond the intrinsic capability of the human body. With the *Ear Pipes* he's toying with an idea derived from a chapter in Gulliver's Travels: the one where Gulliver woke up as a giant, with ears that would have to be much further apart than they were before. He is interested to know how differently the world would sound if our ears were two metres away from one another.

Yayoi Kusama's work, *Narcissus Garden*, was similarly concerned with the nature – and the limitations – of human perception. Involving hundreds of large silver balls, it was an installation you could walk into as it reflected countless images of yourself back to you. It drew you in and then pushed you out again, suggesting that all experience, artistic and otherwise, is about imaginative projection. There's a sense of melancholy in this work, perhaps derived from an apprehension of this fact of life, and also its reference to the myth of Narcissus, dying as he dived into the image of himself. Like many Japanese artists, Kusama is preoccupied with mortality. Likewise, On Kawara – with whom, incidentally, Kusama shared a studio in New York during the 1960s – is equally counting days down, towards eventual death, as he counts them up. For *Pure Consciousness*, in the context of a classroom inhabited by small children, the message of the date paintings is particularly hard.

Tatsuo Miyajima is another artist who was in the Hayward show. He is concerned with endless counting, with the use of digital technology and informed by an ascetic Buddhist philosophy. At the same time, he has a very strong interest in audience participation. This image of his installation *Floating Time* is particularly poignant because in it we see a person trying to catch a number – in a video projection – that is constantly moving

Here is a slide of the work of Makoto Nomura, a musician working very much within a visual arts context. He encouraged visitors to the Hayward to join in with his improvised music. There was a band of Japanese musicians with him but anybody could pick up one of the musical instruments lying around and play with them. At the same time, he was asking visitors to leave contact details if they wanted him and the band to play music in their homes at a later date. It was a remarkable work, generous, like much of the best work now being made by artists from South East and Northern Asia.

Incidentally, it's interesting that the recent biennial in Istanbul, organised by the Japanese curator Yuko Hasegawa, was called 'Egofugal'. It strongly reflects this current tendency to let go, to involve others in artistic experience, to be less precious about artistic authorship. It is manifested also in the way many artists are thinking about how their work occupies space.

In the light of this, at Ikon Gallery we have developed a continuous off-site programme with its own dedicated curator: somebody on our programming team who is only concerned with presenting artwork outside the Ikon Gallery building. In this slide, for example, we see the *Cucumber Journey* by Japanese artist Shimabuku. He made a journey for this by narrowboat along the Grand Union Canal, from behind Chisenhale Gallery in London's East End to Brindley Place, the area in Birmingham where Ikon is located, and capitalised on its slowness. He started with vegetables and various other basic ingredients, and using recipes that were passed on by his crew of volunteers, he arrived at Ikon with dozens of jars of pickles. These were consumed as a feast at an opening reception at Ikon.

This work by Simon Patterson is called *Manned Flight*. It is an installation of an old Second World War surveillance kite – one that can actually lift a human being – which suggests a crash into the façade of Baskerville House in the centre of Birmingham. On the kite are inscribed the words 'Yuri Gagarin' and so it becomes a carrier for an idea of the tragic Russian astronaut, and more generally, for the fallacies of hope epitomised by the story of Icarus. The work of Cornelia Parker similarly combines references to oblivion and the everyday – as seen previously in *Cold Dark Matter* with its solar system revolving around a light bulb. Here is a fireworks display which she set off from the roof of Birmingham's landmark Rotunda Building and, incidentally, it was the first project in our current off-site programme. The pyrotechnic mixture included a pulverised meteorite so that, as they exploded over the city centre, the fireworks created a meteorite shower. The next step in this work, yet to come, will be the placement of various plaques around Birmingham's market area declaring that on a particular day in early April 2000, a meteorite fell on Birmingham.

It would be wrong to suggest that at Ikon we are fixated simply with presenting artwork outdoors. Sometimes we do 'fieldwork' with artists in preparation for gallery exhibitions, as with Gillian Wearing's *Broad Street*. This video installation (2001), depicts the extraordinary cathartic activity that occurs every Friday and Saturday night around the clubs and bars in Birmingham – as it also does, allegedly, in Newcastle – most intensely between the hours of nine p.m. and three a.m., before a sad and drunken conclusion. And finally, this slide is from Ceal Floyer's exhibition at Ikon at the beginning of last year. By contrast, it was very quiet and minimal, provoking a strong negative audience response – paradoxically, because the artist could not have been more sympathetic to a sceptical response to art. Certainly she is very ambivalent about what it means to be an artist. One room in the exhibition contained only a little A4 sheet of card with a (Tom and Jerry) mouse hole drawn on it, propped up between the floor and wall facing the entrance. It was a funny, modest expression of an impulse to get out of the gallery.

(Audience applause)

LAURA GODFREY ISAACS:

Thank you. As the introduction said, I've been running projects from within my house for the last three years. And what I'm going to do today, because I was asked to give a short presentation, is to present three projects to you, which I hope will articulate some of the issues that

I'm trying to deal with by setting up the project. As was also said, I was a practising artist myself up until I started the project HOME. There were a lot of reasons why I decided to set up the project. Some were personal and some were kind of political with a small 'p'. My own practice as an artist was very concerned with gender issues and latterly, with domestic craft. The last work that I made actually involved knitting and sewing. So issues around the domestic were very pertinent to me as an artist. Also, I'd always been involved in curating my own and other people's work, and had always been very interested in the dynamics of how my work was contextualised by curators and institutions. I had very often been unhappy with the way that a lot of my own work had been curated and felt that I understood the dynamics of how exhibitions were put together. I wasn't always happy with how they were happening and therefore wanted to, and was interested to, take that control myself as an artist.

Then there were other, personal reasons that, in some ways, were involved with actually renovating this particular house which, over a two and a half year period, became a really important creative process for me. The idea of creating a home, of home-making, was very, very interesting to me and it actually became more interesting to me than making my own practice in the studio. So when the house was finished and I moved in with my family, it seemed like it was something waiting to happen and that it really needed the rest of the story to happen and so I started running the projects. I was also quite happy to stop working as an artist myself and had felt that I had come to the end of what I wanted to say in that particular way of practising. So even though I don't call myself an artist any more, because I don't make work, I still think like an artist and I'm not sure if I'm really comfortable with being called a curator yet – or ever.

This slide is just to show you what the house looks like from the outside. It's in an ordinary street in Camberwell in South East London. It is quite an interesting house from the outside. It's quite imposing, with this strange turret on the left-hand side. It's double-fronted but nevertheless it exists on a normal street in South East London.

The first project I am going to show you is a performance art project that I did in July 1999 involving twelve artists. This is actually a publicity shot for the project: it's a digital image that's been stitched together to show all of the artists within the domestic space. It's a kind of panorama and the project involved a whole evening for the audience. There were three staged performances that the audience watched together and then, after an interval, there was a series of durational pieces all the way round the house. As you can see, the actual functional spaces of the house are used. There is one space on the top floor – which I'll show you later – which is a notional white space, but generally speaking, all of the functional spaces are used, including the basement, the bathrooms, the bedrooms, the hallways, the kitchen and my daughter's playroom.

This is the back space of the house and this slide is showing you the image of a piece by the performance artist Bobby Baker. She is known and has been known, since the 80s really, as someone who deals with the domestic and family life. The piece that she performed at HOME was called *Table Occasions*. It's a piece that she can adapt to different contexts and in it, she serves an imaginary meal for a group of guests and there are rules set, the most important being that she has to serve the meal standing on the table – she's not allowed to stand on the floor. What you hear is her internal dialogue and her anxieties about the interaction between the guests and her expectations of the event. She becomes increasingly anxious and out of control and the food starts being thrown on the plates and people aren't getting on and the whole thing starts to deteriorate, to the point where she actually dives under the tablecloth and the whole of the dinner party crashes to the ground! That was incredible for the audience because no one was expecting it. They were quite happily going along with this narrative which suddenly gets disrupted – splashes of food all over everybody – and then she continues to dance on the remaining part of the tablecloth, which makes a really nice reference to painting. Bobby was trained as a painter originally and a lot of her work refers to painting. Now you can see with this project that the audience is sitting on benches. In some respects it's being staged almost like a theatre event. Nevertheless, you know they are sitting within the house... the crash of all the crockery, the food splashing everywhere; there's a kind of a surprise and a transgression in it happening within the domestic space. I mean, it is perfectly obvious why someone like Bobby would be exhibiting or producing this work within this context and she herself has opened her own kitchen. She did a piece called *The Kitchen Show* where, over ten nights, she performed a piece in her own kitchen. So when I did this piece it was the first time that I had curated performance work. Bobby is someone that has been a very important artist to me and it was very exciting to have her come and do something in the space.

This is a slide showing the white space on the top floor and this is another piece that was in that show, which the audience were free to wander in and out of. The piece, by the artist Helena Bryant, is called *Slug Woman Makes A Painting*. Again, it's a very nice reference to painting and, I think, to Bobby's work as well. At the beginning of the piece the artist is in a sort of plastic sheet and is blindfolded. There's a slowed down soundtrack and over about a forty-five minute period, the artist wriggles around on this canvas and knocks over the paint and, as she calls it, makes this slow-motion action painting. It's quite a sharp piece looking at the macho gestures of painting: she's completely lowly and abject and the piece itself becomes muddy and all the colours lose their purity from the very beginning. So it's a very abject piece, in which the artist becomes completely covered in paint. It's exciting for me to have work presented that perhaps makes a very strong reference to the domestic, to family life and the everyday but, nevertheless, also to show work that is completely unexpected so that you go into a house and see this work that is, in a way, very transgressive of the space.

This slide shows a third piece from that project by a performance artist called Joshua Sofaer. He performed in the bedroom and made this sort of tent-like structure over the bed from which he performs, but he also used it as a way to project images. Again, people are crammed into the bedroom. He had made this amazing dress which is covered in paint samples and then he also sung Joseph and the Technicolour Dreamcoat, but with slightly changed lyrics. It's a very humorous piece. What I discovered about doing this show, which was really well received by the audience, was how successful it was presenting performance work in this context. Obviously, performance work itself, its history, has always dealt with context and has sought spaces outside of institutional art spaces, has tried to get away from the commodification of art, to engage with the everyday, and is about interaction with the audience. And so the sort of process for the audience, coming into a real house, a space that is semi-private, witnessing something together which also presents a sort of social context for the audience, is a very good marriage. This project was very important for me in the sense that I've now gone on to specialise in performance work. But having said that,

I'm going to show you some other projects.

Even if one is using a domestic space which seems to suggest that things will be discrete and subtle and exclusively to do with the domestic in terms of subject matter, there's plenty of scope, I believe, for making some quite spectacular interventions. This project was a case in point. It's a project by the artist Elizabeth Wright, who normally deals very much with the idea of scale in her work. Her pieces are either very much larger or smaller than everyday objects and so by changing the scale of an object she creates this uncertainty and she's very interested in ideas of the uncanny. I asked her to do a project in the house and gave her a completely open brief. That's generally how I work with artists: to present the house as a site and allow them to do whatever they want so long as it doesn't damage the building. So what she decided to do was to bring a full-size Volkswagen Caddy Van into the sitting room. We got VW to sponsor the show. I think it was quite a gift for them, because they were saying that they are always trying to get their cars into art spaces for promotions, so they were absolutely delighted when someone came to them and said, 'Could we do it?' So they were very accommodating! This van fitted beautifully into the space with just enough room for the audience to walk around. It had the same kind of dynamic as a lot of her work, in the sense that it was an everyday object which, by altering its position, by changing its context, was completely altered; its meaning was completely altered. This room actually sits on the road, so for the artist it was also a question of moving, by several metres, what was an ordinary object that you would otherwise walk past, so that it was completely transformed.

I'll show you one other exhibition, by the performance artist Franko B, who placed all sorts of different objects around the house, used lots of different rooms. I think his work was a really interesting interaction with the space.

Many of the audience just walked straight past some pieces, like these shoes, because they were sited in exactly the place where someone would place shoes in a hallway. Here you can see the motifs of the heart and the cross, which are motifs that he repeatedly uses on found objects. They have personal meaning for him. He spent a period of his childhood in a Red Cross home and so those issues of protection and safety are very pertinent to him personally, as well as obviously being universal symbols. This is the sitting room again, where the van (by Elizabeth Wright) was, and this is a pinball machine, which really operates a bit like an animated diary for him. It's collaged with all sorts of different images that he collects, kind of souvenir objects, and it's fully functional so the audience could interact with it, as was the car.

When people come to see exhibitions like this, which use the whole house, the way that I manage them is to give people a list of what's in each room. Nothing's labelled and there's no invigilation, so there's a kind of a trust involved in that. I think it can be quite intimidating in some respects for people who come into the house, because I think many of the conventions of being a guest in someone's house operate. There's also trust from me that they can walk round the house and that they won't abuse the trust that I put in them. This slide shows my daughter's playroom: a child's table and chair with, again, the familiar motifs. So this room, for instance, which is not tidied up or sanitised, is a functional space that my daughter uses and artists that want to use this space have, to a certain extent, to negotiate with her – through me, obviously – about whether they can place an object in the space or not.

I think that one of the interesting things about using a private or a semi-private space, not only for the artist but for me as a notional curator, is this kind of level of intimacy with artists. People are coming into my house, they're meeting my family and they're having to negotiate these spaces that have all sorts of different sets of ownership over them. Equally the artists, I would hope, get a very high degree of support from me and as much accommodation as possible and they're also welcomed into the space as, not just visitors, but almost like part of the family while they are doing a project.

This is a neon piece by Franko B in the bathroom. We used the bathroom also on one interesting occasion for a one-to-one performance, where Franko B was in the bath and the audience went in one at a time and had about five minutes with him. Leading from the big performance event that I showed you, I've now been running a regular performance evening, which I call a salon, once a month for two years. That's now had about twenty-five different performances and used the house in all sorts of different ways: either the whole audience watch something or they have a one-to-one experience like I've described. And that, in a way, is almost an extension of the big performance event, because calling it a salon obviously indicates that it's a reference to the historical idea of a woman hosting an evening of discussion. People are invited in for the evening, there's a performance and then they are invited to stay afterwards and have drinks, in order to try to encourage a social context and a lot of discussion.

This is a slide of the white room upstairs, in which Franko made this installation. He is known mostly as a performance artist and does performances where he bleeds. He'd done one performance where he walked up and down along a catwalk, the blood was spotted and he made this installation work with the resulting canvas. So he brought a bed up and constructed this bedroom which was a very sublime piece. I think that's the last slide. OK, thanks.

(Audience applause)

ANDREW BURTON:

Thank you very much for those fascinating presentations. Before we open this up to the floor, I would like to ask you both a more general question. This series of talks is called 'The Producers'; it's actually named after Susan Hiller's favourite film, but nonetheless it's been about curatorship, essentially. But both of you have, in a sense, been wary of the term 'curatorship'. Laura, you explicitly said that you didn't see yourself as a curator and Jonathan, you referred to the organisation of shows. Do you not see yourselves as curators and, if so, what kind of distinction would you draw and how would you define your role?

JONATHAN WATKINS:

Well, I'm a curator. It's true, I don't say the word too often, but yes I am a curator – a curator/director really. 'Curator' is an interesting word, originally meaning 'guardian of children and lunatics', which not many people know! Then, of course, 'curator' implies the keeping of something, especially within the context of a permanent collection, which we don't have at Ikon. In fact, I've never been the keeper of anything in that respect, but on the other hand, I'm the keeper of an art institution and the development of the identity of an art institution. So no, I don't have difficulty with the word 'curator', with all its different meanings.

LAURA GODFREY-ISAACS:

It's not that I really have difficulty with it. It's just that, yes, it does have that connotation for me of caring for a collection and also, as I was trying to explain, I do feel more that I'm a facilitator for artists. That's not necessarily how other people might see me, but in my own head I tend to invite artists to do something and then I try and facilitate them to do it. So I think 'facilitator' or 'programmer' probably sits better with me. I was thinking about this on the train because I saw quite a few other people have been asked this question during this series, so I thought it might come up. It made me think about how I used to hate being called a 'painter' or a 'sculptor' or an 'installation artist'. I was always trying to evade those kinds of terms. I think it's also because I'm always interested in things that can't be defined, so I don't really like to be defined myself and what interests me often are things that also can't be defined. That's probably why I like a lot of performance work, because it is kind of formless or hard to define. But if people want to call me a curator, if that's how they see me, that's fine.

ANDREW BURTON:

But neither of you deal with amassing collections, which is also going to be the situation at BALTIC, which is not going to have a collection. Do you find that a liberating experience: not to have to acquire works and keep them?

JONATHAN WATKINS:

Not particularly. I mean, I like the idea that one day I might be working with a collection. It would be an experience that I'd quite like to have. I don't have difficulty with it, but then on the other hand, I'm not straining to have a collection to work with either.

LAURA GODFREY-ISAACS:

I've worked with collections as an artist, doing educational projects and workshops. I think you can work very dynamically with a collection, but I wouldn't want to be in that institutional position myself – not at the moment.

ANDREW BURTON:

Are there questions from the audience?

QUESTION:

In what way do you see yourselves as protecting the artists or people that you work with? I got the sense you had a kind of protective role.

LAURA GODFREY-ISAACS:

I think if you ask an artist to do something and you set up a situation in which they're going to be putting their trust in you to be professional and create a context for them, then there is also a responsibility to make sure that you do things right and that you put things across to the public in the way that they want them to be put across. You also have a responsibility to the audience to create a high quality experience for them. So a lot of trust and thought needs to go into the whole project.

ANDREW BURTON:

It's an interesting question, particularly in the sense that you're not in a gallery situation where there are now all sorts of protocols which are laid down about how a gallery might work with an artist, with regards to payment and so on. (To Laura Godfrey-Isaacs) How do you find that works in a very different situation?

LAURA GODFREY-ISAACS:

Well, I do pay artists. I've now got funding, so I'm in a position to pay them. I've certainly done things where I didn't have public funding and approached people and asked them if they would do something on that basis. In terms of protecting artists, that's quite key for me when working with someone like Franko B for example, whose work can very easily be sensationalised by the press. So

I think if you're handling that kind of work you have to be incredibly responsible to the artist and hopefully you try to protect the integrity of their work.

JONATHAN WATKINS:

The idea of protecting artists in particular doesn't really interest me. It is a question simply of dealing with people with integrity, with the kind of directness and transparency that I was referring to before. I would like to think that it was there in my relationships with artists but also in my relationship with the audience. So, the idea that one would protect an artist as if they had a special kind of sensibility that needed that...

COMMENT FROM AUDIENCE:

Or as if they were children and lunatics...

JONATHAN WATKINS:

Exactly! I don't like that idea, particularly. In fact, if I were an artist, I'd find it slightly patronising.

COMMENT FROM AUDIENCE:

I think that was the point of my question, actually.

QUESTION:

Can I just pick up on something? Jonathan, I seem to remember, maybe about as much as fifteen years ago, you wrote an article for *Art Monthly*, a polemical piece about curating as an artistic practice , which produced a flurry of letters at the time.

I was just wondering, in connection with Laura's practice, whether you've changed your view on that?

JONATHAN WATKINS:

I've definitely changed my view to a large extent because I wrote that before I was actually working as a curator. It was my observation from the outside, before I started working at Chisenhale. I was teaching art history and writing then – making observations on very conventional ideas of curatorial practice – and didn't fully understand the opportunities for collaboration between curators and artists. I had developed this idea of the work of art as a readymade and to some extent the space and activity around a work of art was sort of an 'aiding of the readymade'. Now I know it's more complicated than that.

The idea of the curator as artist or the artist as curator is interesting in relation to a Russian artist, Vladimir Arkhipov, whom we are working with shortly at Ikon. He was a sculptor in Moscow who decided that the kinds of inventive things that people do in their everyday lives were so much more interesting than his own sculptural work. For example, if someone needed a doormat in Soviet Russia and there were none in the shops that year, they might nail bottletops to planks of wood in order to create an object that did the same job. He decided to stop making sculpture in order to become an artist/collector, a curator as keeper in fact, because he was acquiring a collection of everyday DIY inventions. I'm very interested in the blurring which increasingly occurs between what is done by curators, artists and audiences. But on the other hand, I do think it's useful that we have these terms, using different labels no matter how arbitrary the categories 'artist', 'curator' and 'audience' are. I believe, at this point in history, it is still useful having the idea of art.

ANDREW BURTON:

Laura, that blur between being an artist and a curator has played out in a very particular way for you. Has it been a creative experience?

LAURA GODFREY-ISAACS:

Well as I said, I don't call myself an artist anymore because I don't make work anymore, but I probably do still think like an artist, but then I don't know how a curator thinks, because I'm not a curator – or at least that's not my training, so I don't know. I mean, I don't really see any problem with it; I don't see why artists shouldn't curate work. I don't really think there's an issue. If they want to curate and they do good shows, then great.

JONATHAN WATKINS:

I don't think that artists think differently to curators. Personally, I don't think that artists think differently to anybody else.

LAURA GODFREY-ISAACS:

How can we know that?

QUESTION:

I was just trying to figure out a way that we might be able to know it but I'm going to formulate this in my head as I go along in the manner that an artist, or possibly a curator, would. The question to Jonathan would be: do you ever have an idea for a work that you could just as well make yourself and you end up having to find an artist to do it? I've been an artist and a curator and I've occasionally had to speak to someone and say, 'I've had an idea for your work.' You must, every now and then, have an intervention in the gallery which you could just as easily make yourself: for instance, opening the office door.

And then for Laura the question would be: you know every now and then you get to a point in your life when you do something that's so simple and clear and obvious that you can't go back from it? You couldn't really go back to doing shows in other contexts. I'm overdoing that point, but what I suppose I mean is that the thing that you're doing is now very clear for you, I think, and people make a fuss about it, but it's actually a very straightforward, obvious thing to be doing. The real question is, 'why there are galleries in the world rather than houses that have art?' That's the obvious question, you know, when you give such a clear presentation.

LAURA GODFREY-ISAACS:

I think it is very clear to me why I'm doing what I'm doing and it makes a lot of sense. To me, I think, intellectually or theoretically, the project really is to do with the idea of living with art. In some ways I think it does beg the question, 'Why do there need to be galleries?' and it's in some respects a regret that art has been separated from life, even though artists have been trying to pull it back ever since that happened. But, nevertheless, as I was trying to explain with the white space, I do have a notional gallery space in the house and I have found that it is incredibly useful to have a space like that: an empty space which artists can come into and transform. It's got less of a loaded meaning, even though it's got the meaning of the gallery, but as opposed to using a bathroom or a kitchen or a space that's also got someone else's personal identity stamped on it. So that, in a way, led me back to thinking, well, actually galleries do have a function for artists.

QUESTION:

But the proportion of it is that you have seven rooms that have a function and one gallery?

LAURA GODFREY-ISAACS:

Yes.

QUESTION:

That's a good proportion! Jonathan?

JONATHAN WATKINS:

The question is, could I have an idea that would be identical to or resembles that which an artist could have?

QUESTION:

Yes.

JONATHAN WATKINS:

Absolutely. But it wouldn't be called art.

QUESTION:

Would you do it and then put it on as a show in the space that you curate?

JONATHAN WATKINS:

As an artist?

QUESTION:

I don't really care – just put it in the space. For instance, the two Serpentine shows, which obviously came at key moments in the process of the building: to some extent, you could have devised them. Now, you wouldn't do it because you wouldn't do it. Why wouldn't you do it? Do you see what I mean? Why not? Because that's not your role? Does there always have to be an artist to make that intervention?

JONATHAN WATKINS:

Yes.

QUESTION:

Why?

JONATHAN WATKINS:

I don't think, for example, that there's any intrinsic difference between the creativity of a Russian DIY inventor and Vladimir Arkhipov. The only thing that is different is the context. The artist is not the person who made the object, and it doesn't matter. It's Arkhipov, as an artist, who took it to the 'art place'. I don't have that identity so I couldn't do it, and I wouldn't particularly want to do it.

LAURA GODFREY-ISAACS:

I think you should keep a line there. Having been on both sides – the artist and the curator/organiser – from my own experience, I definitely feel curating/organising is an incredibly creative thing to do. It's not making art, but it's very, very creative. That, for me, is the satisfaction in it; that satisfies me as an artist. It's a very creative thing; it's exciting. You bring the artists together and you're shaping something, making it happen.

QUESTION:

Because the two identities aren't really separate?

LAURA GODFREY-ISAACS:

But I think you have to be. I feel that you have to know what your role is within that negotiation or within that equation and the other part of that equation is the audience. Ultimately the audience is the most important thing. Whatever you're creating is experienced by other people. That's also one of the reasons that I decided to make it very clear to myself and others, if they were interested, that I'm not a practising artist any more.

When I'm doing HOME my role is the organiser or the curator, not the artist, because I feel it's much clearer to do that and, I think, happier for everyone else involved in it as well.

JONATHAN WATKINS:

The problem is also with the idea of art being creative, because art obviously isn't always very creative. That's Arkhipov's point. Very often things that aren't art can be a lot more creative than art.

LAURA GODFREY-ISAACS:

Sure.

JONATHAN WATKINS:

I've just been judging an art prize and I've seen something like six hundred entries in two days and you know, an awful lot of art is awful – but, without question, it's still art. Calling it art doesn't mean it's more creative or better than some other expressive gesture that somebody else makes. It's just that it exists within this art category. I mean, this was absolutely the point of my Sydney Biennale or the programme at Ikon and I think Laura's movement around the machine of the art world also suggests that. You don't have to be in the art world to be creative. Some of the most creative people in the world aren't artists and some of the most boring people are!

LAURA GODFREY-ISAACS:

That's also going back to what I was saying, that the creative aspect of making a home was also finding all the creative activities that go on within a home, be they cooking or gardening or creating a child's birthday party. It's like all these creative acts within everyday life are very, very precious acts and somehow, I think, also locating art back within that context which often amplifies those activities, creates a kind of circular conversation.

COMMENT FROM AUDIENCE:

You seem to be very concerned about distinguishing between artists and curators and very clear about who is in which role. You seem to be stepping on almost everyone else's toes around there. I mean, there are architects, interior designers, stage designers, and it seems to me, as an architect, that you're moving into a whole range of different fields of expertise.

JONATHAN WATKINS:

But artists are moving aren't they? All over the place! Cornelia Parker, for example, all of a sudden became an expert on plastic explosives, and then fireworks and meteorites. Franko B is very involved with the world of medicine. The wonderful thing about visual art is how free it is: it can be anything and can move into any territory.

QUESTION:

But what about the old notion of skill that goes with the more traditional demarcation of jobs?

LAURA GODFREY-ISAACS:

One of the mistakes, in a way, of a lot of contemporary art for me has been this kind of inward-looking argument which is all about the debates within art. I'm making huge generalisations, but I find that whole area of practice very frustrating, very insular, very circular, not concerned with the audience, to do with making internal jokes. I'm much more interested in work that engages with the real world and some of those issues are to do with skills. You know, does one need to have a skill to be an artist, which is quite a traditional idea? Or they can work with people who fabricate objects for them and so they start engaging with industry and all sorts of other professionals and I think that's a really exciting way to operate as an artist. It doesn't, in my view, denigrate other disciplines. It shows artists' active interest in other disciplines and their desire to engage outside of internal debates about abstraction.

QUESTION:

I'm more interested in quality rather than the denigration of other disciplines. I just wondered how you judge quality? For example, looking at the way that you interfered with a gallery, as an architect I might have views about that. As an actor or a stage designer you might have views about the quality of the performance, so I just wonder how you will judge quality in this kind of situation?

JONATHAN WATKINS:

But there's no way of quantifying artistic quality.

QUESTION:

No, no, I understand that, but we still operate on notions of quality.

JONATHAN WATKINS:

That is the difficulty for visual art particularly, I think, and that's why an artist like Ceal Floyer gets such stick. It didn't seem to a lot of our visitors, for example, that there was any skill involved in making that little drawing of a mouse hole. On the other hand, there are ways of telling if a building is built properly or not, or if somebody can dance well or can play music in tune or sing – there's a kind of skill involved in such art forms which usually distinguishes artists from others. Visual art doesn't involve such skill, and certainly there's an idea that anybody could do it. Anybody could do that mouse hole, but rather than regarding this as a fundamental problem, actually we would rather celebrate the fact. This inclusive tendency in contemporary art practice – signified by what Laura's doing too – gives reasons for optimism.

QUESTION:

Laura, I've got quite a few questions for you but I will restrict myself to only one at this stage relating to the audience. Do you actually need an audience, except your own family? What I mean is, I think it's a wonderful idea, it's like the king in the 16th century or whenever, who invites a performer to perform in front of his court. It's great, but I mean, what do you need the audience for at all?

LAURA GODFREY-ISAACS:

Well, the artists need the audience, don't they? The artists don't come and do something just to entertain me and my family. They do it because it's an opportunity to make a new piece of work that, nine times out of ten, is going to be funded, it's going to be promoted, it's hopefully going to get some press interest: they're going to get an audience to see their work.

QUESTION:

Why, if that is the case, does the audience need to come into your house?

LAURA GODFREY-ISAACS:

They don't need to do anything. They choose to obviously, because they're interested in what the artist is doing or the context. Hopefully what is then delivered to them is a high-quality experience in terms of the investment the artist has made in the project and the investment that I have made in realising a project and making it open to people.

QUESTION:

Having secured funding, do you find that it's actually restricting the freedom that you have within the space?

LAURA GODFREY-ISAACS:

I haven't really found that yet, particularly. I have had funding from institutions from the first project. The first projects were funded by the institution where I was teaching – it was research funding – so I have always had accountability to somebody. I didn't receive London Arts funding until this year and they've now funded me twice so I'm getting a lot of support, which is brilliant. My main feeling of responsibility is always that towards the artist and towards the audience, and I don't think it's altered that. To go back to what you were saying about why would anyone bother coming to a house in Camberwell to see something. I'm aware of the fact that it takes more effort for somebody to come and see something in a house in Camberwell than it does to stroll down to Tate Modern. I'm aware of that and therefore anxious on my own part and the artist's part to present something that's going to be a very fulsome experience for the audience.

COMMENT FROM AUDIENCE:

I'm thinking about the exhibition 'Chambres d'Amis' in Ghent (1986) when quite well known artists were invited to exhibit in the houses of the inhabitants of the city of Ghent. As a visitor to the exhibition, you would go through this strange motion of becoming like a visitor to homes and gardens, like in the Chelsea Flower Show. It's a very strange thing to go into the lived domestic space to see an exhibition. It's very interesting. I'm not quite sure if I'm formulating a question here, but it's this sort of voyeurism of going into someone's domestic space, and they have not vacated.

ANDREW BURTON:

We've got time for one more question.

QUESTION:

Just to take that slightly further, the Canadian playwright Wallace Shawn wrote a play called 'The Fever' which was designed to be taken around houses and performed in people's living rooms. You were then invited on to the next house, but it was the host's responsibility to invite the audience, so it wasn't like the public coming into your space. So how do you see your project evolving, expanding? Are you literally going to keep it as it is or can we invite the performers to our houses and invite our own audience to see performances – a similar kind of thing?

LAURA GODFREY-ISAACS:

I'm not entirely sure how it's going to evolve over the long term. I know what I'm doing over the next eighteen months. I think the way it's evolving is to carry on running a programme in the house as I've been doing, but I'm also starting to devise performance and more shows that start in a house and then tour to other venues. For instance, I'm doing a project that's going to be called 'The Kitchen' where five performance artists will do individual pieces, but it will be more like a show in the kitchen. That piece will then tour to other kitchens, which could be other domestic kitchens, they could be institutional kitchens, they could be temporary kitchens set up in theatre or gallery spaces. So I'm starting to devise things that start in the context of the house but then have a life afterwards. I also work as a kind of curator or consultant organising projects for other people in domestic or other lived spaces. So, I will continue to run my own programme but can also be hired out to do things for other people.

ANDREW BURTON:

That seems a particularly intriguing note to close with. Thank you both very much indeed for coming to Newcastle.

(Audience applause)

THE PRODUCERS: CONTEMPORARY CURATORS IN CONVERSATION

6 MARCH 2002, UNIVERSITY OF NEWCASTLE, DEPARTMENT OF FINE ART

JAMES PUTNAM AND BARBARA LONDON IN CONVERSATION CHAIRED BY RICHARD DEACON

SUSAN HILLER:

Hello and welcome to the fourteenth event in 'The Producers' series. Future 'Producers' sessions will be held at BALTIC rather than here at the University. I'd now like to introduce the participants in today's discussion. First of all, Barbara London, who is the associate curator in film and video at the Museum of Modern Art in New York where she has worked since the mid-seventies. Barbara founded the Museum's ongoing new media exhibition programme in which she has created a platform for artists such as Laurie Anderson, Gary Hill, Joan Jonas and Nam June Paik. In addition to the ongoing exhibition programme, she also established the Video Study Center at MoMA, which documents and preserves work in this field and which holds a unique collection of independent artists' videos and related publications. Barbara is also a writer: she's written widely on video and media art, and you can read some of her curatorial dispatches on the MoMA website.

James Putnam is a curator at the British Museum in London. He has initiated a number of unusual and innovative contemporary art exhibitions starting, in 1994, with an exhibition called 'Time Machine: Ancient Egypt and Contemporary Art', where artists such as Marc Quinn and Andy Goldsworthy made work which was displayed within the British Museum's Egyptian Galleries. James has written both on ancient Egyptian art and contemporary art and his recent book, *Art and Artifact: The Museum as Medium*, is a survey of the relationship between the artist and the museum, from the beginnings of what we now think of as museums in the cabinets of curiosity, to the portable museums of Marcel Duchamp, and on to contemporary artists.

The chair today is our first ever guest chair: Richard Deacon has been kind enough to assume this role today. Richard is one of Britain's best known and most significant contemporary sculptors and is also a member of the Board of Trustees of BALTIC. He's exhibited extensively abroad and in this country and has had major solo exhibitions at the Whitechapel Art Gallery, Tate Liverpool and many other places. At the moment there's a work of Richard's on exhibit locally at the Laing Art Gallery, in 'Life is Beautiful' which some of you will undoubtedly be seeing this week. So, that's all from me and now over to Richard.

RICHARD DEACON:

Thank you Susan. This evening we have two curators from two very venerable and major institutions – the Museum of Modern Art in New York and the British Museum in London. They, of course, have different roles within those two institutions. The evening is going to run according to the usual format. I'll ask each of the speakers to make a presentation of about fifteen or twenty minutes and after that I'll put some questions to them both. Then I'll throw it open to the floor and hope that you also have questions. Undoubtedly there's an audience here who may well have seen fourteen out of fourteen 'Producers', and have significant comparative questions to ask. The decision as to who goes first and who goes second was really based on the antiquity of the institutions to which our two speakers belong. James is going to speak first since the British Museum does predate the Museum of Modern Art and Barbara is going to follow. So, it's over to you James.

JAMES PUTNAM:

Hi. I'm going to try something that's a bit of an experiment. Susan mentioned this book that I've just done called *Art and Artifact: The Museum as Medium* and I have a selection of slides that go along with this. Obviously there's no time to talk about all of them, but I'll run through them continuously, without comment, on the left screen while I talk about a different selection, which I'll show simultaneously on the other screen. The slides I'll talk around will be curatorial projects that I've done which fit in more appropriately with this 'Producers' series, but on the other hand, the *Museum as Medium* slides give a kind of colour or character to what I believe in and what I do in the sense of combining contemporary art with the historical. So, it might work or it might not. If it doesn't, I'll stop it as you may be bombarded with too many images at once. So let's see what happens.

First I'll give you a bit of background about myself. I started off by studying art history and I specialised in Renaissance art. Then I went on to do Egyptology at the British Museum and for many years was working within the Egyptian Department. For a long time I was immersed in, and carried away with, the whole history of the Museum and the fabulous sense of antiquity that it all had, and was studying Egyptian art. Familiarity with its great sculpture gallery – one of the finest rooms in the world displaying Egyptian sculpture – made me feel really inspired to do something there: inject a presence of the contemporary into the space, indirectly subverting the linear notion of time and history.

So, I did this exhibition that Susan mentioned, called 'Time Machine', where I worked with a dozen artists, international ones mainly, to bring in, to actually create projects, in that gallery. A lot of the artists really responded to the space and the dynamics of Egyptian sculpture. This is a work by Andy Goldsworthy (*Sandwork*). It involved thirty tons of sand which had to be brought into the gallery from basement level. In character with a lot of later things I've done there, it combined the site of the museum as an architectural space, and the artist bringing in something new to that space.

This was a work created specially by Marc Quinn, called *Rubber Soul*, which involved a frozen hibernating frog: a particular type of tree frog that goes to sleep in the winter and it is able to survive in sub-zero temperatures and then come to life again in the spring. So this tied in with the duration of the exhibition, which was on for about three months, and it also fitted well with the Egyptian concept of mummification. I went on to curate another version of that exhibition in the Museo Egizio in Turin a year later (1995) which involved a different selection of artists. This work is by Kiki Smith, called *Southern Hemisphere Constellation* and we used most of the existing museum vitrines and it was very much, as I said before, a combination of the site with the artists' installations, thereby creating something different.

This slide is a work called *Tree Door* by Giuseppe Penone. He didn't actually make this work specially, but it was the first time it was shown and he completed it for the show. The nice thing about this is that it's made from the same cedar wood as the Egyptian mummy cases and other artifacts displayed with it in the gallery.

From 'Time Machine' I went on to work on a number of intervention projects also in the British Museum's Egyptian Gallery. This slide shows *Questions of Taste* by Richard Wentworth. It was part of a wider multi-site project in 1997 called 'Collected', which was curated by the artist Neil Cummings for the Photographer's Gallery, London. As part of that I worked directly with Richard Wentworth and Fred Wilson to create installations within the Egyptian Gallery. This was, in fact, a collection of drinks containers taken from all the rubbish bins in and around the British Museum which were juxtaposed with ancient Egyptian drinking vessels, some of them dating back to about 4,000 B.C. The nice thing about it was that Richard Wentworth took on board the whole notion of museum practice by labelling all the drinks containers in a totally museological way. For instance, the label might say something like, 'Seven Laminate Polycarbonate Bottles, Inscribed Oasis. Found on the British Museum Steps, 3rd June 1997'. And all these matched the conventional British Museum labels on the other side.

We really liked the idea that museum visitors could relate in some way to the ancient Egyptians more as people rather than as some far-removed ancient civilization. So we found a nice quote from an ancient Egyptian papyrus all about beer drinking which we translated and ran on a label on the other side. There are other nice little connections we made: this was, as you can see, a plastic Coke bottle that we found in one of the basements of the museum that had been perforated to use as a sprinkler. There's a lot of dust in the museum and the cleaner went round and sprinkled water, so this was labelled accordingly by Richard Wentworth: 'Plastic Coke Bottle Adapted for use as a Sprinkler', or there was another one: 'Polystyrene Cup Adapted for use as an Ashtray'. All these little things actually told us a lot about contemporary culture, if you like, and the bottom line of it had various drinks containers that had been run over or flattened so they assumed an almost archaeological appearance. The interesting thing is, as soon as the glass was put on the vitrine, everything became more bona fide and authentic – otherwise it looked merely like a lot of old rubbish. People started looking at it in a totally different way and obviously that's the basis on which museum devices render objects more precious.

I've done some projects in other museum spaces, including an ongoing series at the Freud Museum. [Slide] This was a show with Sophie Calle in Freud's house which we called 'Appointment' (1999). This is her wedding dress on the famous couch and there were other objects belonging to her which, in a sense, constituted a collection – her own personal museum. If any of you know Sophie Calle's work, she usually writes very succinct texts that go alongside the objects that have narratives within them. We put a little pink label alongside each of the objects in her collection and it fitted in really well with a lot of Freud's psychoanalytical theories.

I've also done projects in non-museum spaces. This was a show at The Roundhouse, London, with the work of Mimmo Paladino and Brian Eno (*I Dormienti or The Sleepers*, 1999). It was the first time that the undercroft of the Roundhouse, which is a fantastic space, had ever been used for an art show. It's a bit like a catacomb or a labyrinth and people could walk around in the space and hear this specially created music by Brian Eno which was his typical kind of ambient sound, but it was ever-evolving. There were twelve different CD players that were playing simultaneously on random/shuffle mode and all the tracks blended with each other in a montage of sound.

Another project I did at the Freud Museum in 2000 was with Sarah Lucas called 'Beyond the Pleasure Principle', after Freud's book of the same name. There again it was a kind of combination of Sarah Lucas' work, and the mind and house of Freud. She made some new work specially for the show: this sculpture is actually called *Beyond the Pleasure Principle* (2000) and it inspired her to go on and produce a whole new series of work after the show. This work was acquired by the Tate Gallery afterwards and it was actually the fruits of us driving around the weekend before, picking up various bits of old furniture and stuff like that and putting them together for the exhibition. When displayed in the Tate Gallery it will never have quite the same power as when installed in its original intended context of Freud's house

What might be a bit different about the projects that I do is the fact that they often rely totally on historical material. The idea of the museum as a medium in itself is, I think, a fundamental part of what I do. At the British Museum I've started this Contemporary Arts and Cultures programme – as I call it – which is not actually limited to visual art. The first residency we had was with the dancer/choreographer Michael Clark, who worked with myself and other museum curators to study different pieces of sculpture in the museum. He was very interested in the idea of gesture and how that could be used and went on later to develop this theme as part of his subsequent work, although we didn't actually stage a performance at the museum. Then we did a residency with João Penalva, funded by Sci-Art, which was based on the artist observing and documenting the conservation department at the Museum and the idea of the museum obsessively preserving things that weren't necessarily meant to be preserved by the culture that created them.

I've also worked a bit with the Henry Moore Institute taking selections from the British Museum Collection up to Leeds and installing them in a very different way than they would be shown at the British Museum. I've also organised artists' performances: we did one with Tracey Emin last year, in fact. I say she did a 'performance' – it was very much her not talking about her work but just being her. I think it was different having her do that in the British Museum, where she didn't feel as self-conscious as she might at the Tate Gallery, or somewhere where she had to talk about her work. We framed it around the theme of Cleopatra, the major British Museum exhibition on at the time, and Tracey had just returned from Egypt and showed slides of her Nile cruise. It was her being completely open with the audience and really enjoying the special atmosphere of the Museum.

My feeling generally is that the British Museum – and you can probably see this from some of the images I've shown – is a great working medium and a real inspiration for artists. More and more we've seen artists using the vitrine, the plinth and the label as an integral part of their work, but also as a way of examining the museum as an institution that presents an autonomous view of history. Also some artists have taken a more critical stance, mimicking or contesting this role. There is now a frequent tendency for artists to make installations or 'interventions' in museum spaces and artists being invited to curate exhibitions; artists actually re-hanging permanent collections and the whole idea that artists are coming in to somehow reanimate old collections and bring different audiences into the museum. I also found this quite a challenge at the British Museum which, as you can imagine, is in some ways one of the most conservative institutions that you could find. It's been, I guess, a pretty difficult challenge to carry on this kind of work within an institution which is by its nature very fixed and rigid. It has all its different departments, its different agendas, which are very much part of its organisation. In 2003 we're celebrating 250 years of the British Museum as a great public museum, so my feeling about what I do there is also to revive the idea of the museum as a more philosophical institution like it was once intended to be. So it shouldn't necessarily be a place that only looks backwards but it's very much somewhere that should be addressing contemporary culture and representing what is going on in the present.

(Audience applause)

BARBARA LONDON:

Hi. I'm delighted to be here. I want to thank Susan Hiller, Vicki Lewis and Sune Nordgren for inviting me, and for creating a remarkable new venue for contemporary art at BALTIC. I look forward to seeing the opening show in the completed building.

First I'll give you a little anecdote about my background since James talked a bit about his. I was in graduate school studying Islamic art, interested in the trade route between China and the Near East. (Ideas can similarly be transmitted on the backs of camels and over the airwaves.) When I was ready to enter the museum profession, there weren't any curatorial positions open in Islamic art. At that point MoMA opened its doors to me, and I worked first with the International Programme on several exhibitions the Museum circulated abroad. I assisted Jennifer Licht, one of the pioneering MoMA curators who addressed installation as an art form. With her I selected videotapes for the sculpture show 'Some Recent American Art', which went to Australia. Many of the sculptors in the show were working with video, including Lynda Benglis, Richard Serra and Bob Morris, among others.

Then I switched over to a curatorial position in the Department of Prints and Illustrated Books, and from there I started an artists' book collection with works by Ed Ruscha, Sol LeWitt, Gilbert and George, among many others. I always like the hot potatoes!

There was a sort of synchronicity. When the Museum purchased its first video equipment – a playback deck and two monitors – and launched an ongoing video exhibition programme, I was this bright-eyed, bushy-tailed curator who ran with this lively new art form of video. In 1977 the Museum obtained a grant from the Rockefeller Foundation to absolve me of all my Print Department responsibilities, and I started to work exclusively on video.

From my Print Department colleagues, I learned about archiving and paying attention to the details around a particular artwork. I understood how important it was to connect video to what was going on in the larger world of contemporary art. I also saw that individual videotapes would all turn to gummed up globs unless someone saved them and the related ephemera. The Museum started to acquire and preserve video art.

We also launched a monthly lecture series called 'Video Viewpoints' – a bit like 'The Producers', in a way – where artists come and show their work and talk about it. I've always been very dogged about these presentations – I've always told the artists they must discuss as well as show their work. We audiotaped and transcribed each presentation. It means we have an artist like Vito Aconcci speaking at the Museum right after he made *Red Tapes* (1977), which is the last video work he made. We also have Laurie Anderson speaking, after I worked with her on a MoMA 'Projects' show in 1978. A very young Tony Oursler spoke in 1980 soon after he made one of his first tapes called *The Life of Phyllis*. This is a wicked little story spun simply with a TV set made of scrolling paper and a Barbie doll! Currently we're showing Tony's tape at MoMA in a show called 'First Decade'. Many of you are the students here, and you understand the work of your generation the best. But it's very important to consider the issues around work made decades before.

My first slide shows you where I work. This is the façade of MoMA, an iteration from 1939. In the upper right corner is a small sign that reads 'Art in our Time'. MoMA, like the British Museum, has a history, and is an institution with well-honed procedures, run by knowledgeable professionals. Alfred Barr, the first director of MoMA, knew we had to think not only about Picasso, which when we were founded in 1929 was new for New York. He knew that if you're going to be a museum of the 20th century, you must consider the art in our time and what that means historically. The way Barr envisioned fostering, assembling, promoting and exhibiting up-to-date art was to think about the institution as a moving torpedo: a torpedo that moves forward in time. In 1929 Barr and his associates thought we would lop off (give to the Metropolitan Museum) the oldest work as we moved into the future-present. But this strategy really didn't work, because if you're going to make way for the new by getting rid of the old – and of course by that time, these would have become the most valuable works – you've also got to get rid of the expertise of the people there. Do you get rid of your staff as well? Do you get rid of all the research archives that curators have built up and protect, too? We save every artist's bio, photo, catalogue, magazine article and interview! A museum is much more than its permanent collection on view. It's the people who are thinking about the art and moving along with it into the future.

For those of you who are really young and weren't around in the sixties, artists were dealing with television before the portable video camera came onto the market in 1965. This is Nam June Paik's *TV with Candle* (1963). He replaced the insides of a TV set with a simple candle. He is asking the viewer to consider why this particular piece of furniture is so prominently placed in the living room. Why is TV a one-way form of communication? Is TV viewing akin to a meditation on light? Do we participate by putting our own content into it? Of course, the work also asks a lot about what art is, and what our relationship is to these mass media that are so prevalent, so much a part of our life.

When the portable video camera came out, many artists took to the streets and used the medium as a political tool. They thought they would replace television with video and take over the world. It was the anti-Vietnam War movement, it was the beginning of feminism and everything was kind of equal, except it wasn't equal. You could document a demonstration; you could document a sit-in. The equipment was called 'portable', but really the take-up deck weighed about 30lbs. The camera weighed at least 10lbs and you huffed and puffed as you carried the gear and shot.

Back then, the portable video cameras and recording gear generated black and white tapes. Some artists really wanted colour. Nam June manipulated the guts of the TV set and made *TV with Magnet* (1963), a kind of interactive piece. Move the magnet on the top of the set, and this changes the abstract colour pattern. Here was interactivity before there was a name for it.

In the late 1960s, artists were experimenting with new media. Bruce Nauman explored holography, making this *Artist as a Fountain*. He also made this sculpture, called *Hand to Mouth*, out of fiberglass. Of course, many artists live hand to mouth. But it's also about, 'what is perception?' This was a time when artists were working a lot with their bodies, pointing a camera at themselves. Nauman did this brilliant installation in 1968-69 called *Corridor*. It was such a narrow space that when you walked down it, you felt awkward and became very conscious of your own body. At the far end of the corridor there are two stacked monitors, and both of their screens appear to depict images of the empty corridor. One monitor is a pre-recorded image of the space. You realise there's a camera above the entrance behind you, because after you have walked into the space a few steps, suddenly the back of your head appears on one of the monitors. The narcissist in all of us wants to see our face on the monitor. But when you turn around to look at the camera, the moment your head is turned, your face is on the monitor. But you can't flip around fast enough to see yourself. Forget it!

A piece that I showed at MoMA back in 1976 by Peter Campus is called *aen* (1977). You walked into a dark room and headed towards a large rectangle of light on the far wall. As you approached, you stood near a tiny red spotlight sitting on the floor. Suddenly your face was projected splat right on the wall, upside down. It was a very harsh image of yourself. No matter how much you interacted with the image, you couldn't make this dark brooding view of yourself more attractive. An unobtrusive live camera was installed nearby.

Peter was one of the first artists to be invited to produce a videotape at a U.S. public television station. He had begun his career as a filmmaker and was very literate with the tools. The producers knew he would be able to communicate with the engineers and not drive them crazy. He produced this classic tape called *Three Transitions* (1973), which is in the Museum's collection and is on view right now in the 'First Decade' show. Peter used a very simple technique called a soft dissolve. He has two cameras, one on either side of a wall-sized sheet of brown paper, so it appears that he's slicing right through his back and then walking through himself.

William Wegman worked alone in his studio with his alter ego, a Weimaraner dog by the name of Man Ray. His *Selected Works: Reel #3* is so simple, the timing so perfect. The humour catches viewers off guard.

With *Vertical Roll* (1973), Joan Jonas caught viewers off guard in a different way. You might know that early television sets had 'vertical hold' buttons, because images often drifted vertically. As a young girl, I found it frustrating when the Ed Sullivan show with The Beatles drifted upwards endlessly. Today, television sets are more stable and you never see this 'rolling' flaw. In *Vertical Roll* Joan performs with a series of masks, as the frame constantly rolls to a percussive beat (actually, a spoon hitting a tabletop). Ultimately she deconstructs the process when, at the very end of the performance, she comes out in front of the rolling image. Throughout the making of the tape, Joan had one camera directed at her performing and a second camera on the TV set depicting her. Joan's exploration of video's processes related to Richard Serra's questioning of sculpture through his thrown lead pieces.

The next tape is a very short piece by Laurie Anderson, one of her Personal Service Announcements (1987), shot as she stood next to the short-order cook in a New York Greek coffee shop. Those of you from England know the political implications of 'Yankee doodle,' which is not simply a piece of pasta.

(Video plays)

Laurie Anderson: "Recently a lot of people have been talking about changing the national anthem to 'America The Beautiful'. Now I don't believe that's such a great idea. I mean, I really like the 'Star Spangled Banner'. It is kind of hard to sing along with those arpeggios when you're out in the ball park and the bands are singing away and it's sort of pathetic really, watching everybody try to hang on to that melody. The words are great though. Just a lot of questions written during a fire. Things like 'Hey, do you see anything over there?' 'I don't know, there's sort of smoke.' 'Say, isn't that a flame?' 'Hmm, couldn't say really, it's pretty early in the morning.' 'Hey, do you smell something burning?' I mean, that's the whole song. It is a big improvement though over most national anthems which are 4:4 timing: 'We're number one, this is the best place.' I also like the B-side of the national anthem: 'Yankee doodle'. Truly a surrealist masterpiece!

(Background music)

Yankee doodle came to town
Riding on a pony.
Stuck a feather in his hat
And called it macaroni.

Now, if you can understand the words to this song, you can understand anything that's happening in the art world today."

Laurie made films and did performances before she got into music. When she was making a new record in 1987, Warner Brothers asked if she wanted to produce a new music video. Instead she allocated those monies towards these Personal Service Announcements. She was advocating for more federal support for the arts. Her PSAs were aired on cable stations across the U.S.

In 1985 I organised a show called 'Music Video: The Industry and its Fringes,' in which I dealt with the collaborations between musicians and visual artists. I knew that music companies rise and fall, the music directors come and go, and work disappears. Bear in mind that MTV was founded several years before my show, and the field was hot. For the show I obtained a range of music videos, from the Beatles and Captain Beefheart, to Zbigniew Rybczynski and David Byrne. All of the works are now in the MoMA collection. The record companies allowed us to make an archival copy of each work. The 'Music Video' show represents an inventive artistic moment, and one day some of the work might have as much import as, say, the posters Toulouse-Lautrec designed for Paris cabarets. I'm prepared, if you want to argue with me!

Inasmuch as it is always already taking place is Gary Hill's installation that MoMA commissioned in 1991, and later acquired. The work exists as a shelf in a wall. Sixteen television sets have been taken apart and stripped down – exposed are just the picture tubes of varying sizes. Each screen depicts a life-size part of a man's body. It resembles a live still life or a memento mori. The level of the shelf is such that you actually have to bend or bow a little to look. The loop of each body part appears to be unending, so it resembles a live body with rearranged parts. Wires extend from the back of each tube and out the back of the shelf to the hidden chassis of each TV. The wires have the feeling of nerve endings.

What does it mean when an institution like MoMA acquires such an installation? What do I, as a curator, have to think about in terms of the aesthetics of this piece? The technology is fugitive, it's not going to be around for very much longer. Flat screens and small projectors have already replaced TV sets. Should my institution buy one or more sets of each of the various sized *Inasmuchas..* TV tubes? A TV tube has a life like you and me. How should the Museum store the equipment? And the Museum needs to have Gary Hill define what the aesthetics are, so that when he's not around, the Museum can make appropriate decisions about how to retrofit the piece.

Lovers (1995) is a major installation by Teiji Furuhashi, a Japanese artist I knew very well. He founded the Kyoto-based performance/media art group Dumb Type. I followed Teiji's work since he was in art school and tracked his career. This means that over time I accumulated bulging file folders on Teiji. (I have file folders on every artist I've seen. The ephemera is part of our Video Study Center archives, which is open by appointment to scholars.) *Lovers* is a remarkable work: you walk into a room 9 metres by 9 metres, with black walls and a white linoleum floor. A simple metal structure in the middle holds video and slide projectors. Life size, naked figures are projected onto the wall. The spectral figures run and leap very gracefully. Sometimes they merge or overlap in a virtual embrace, and then move on. There's a moment when one of the figures – it's actually the artist – finds you through a motion detector. He stands there, lifts his arms up and falls back into the void. It's called *Lovers* but I think the work is very much about love in the time of Aids. Canon, producers of the work, donated the installation to MoMA, for which we are very grateful. The piece was made with 1995 Mac software that's now obsolete. We need to go back to Teiji's collaborators and upgrade all the computers and the software. This requires preservation monies.

P.S.1 is now affiliated with MoMA and we have a productive relationship. Currently Richard Deacon has an important work in the P.S.1 courtyard. What does it mean for MoMA, a 75 year-old institution, to move forward? P.S.1 was founded in the mid-seventies and occupies a former school. With a small staff, P.S.1 can move very fast: often they put a show together in three months or less. At MoMA we take at least two years to organise a show.

The Museum has embarked on an expansion

programme. We are doubling our spaces. At the end of May we're closing our 53rd Street site for three years and will open a temporary facility in a former factory in Queens, around the corner from P.S.1. We will have 185,000 square feet (25,000 square feet devoted to gallery space). We will present a series of dynamic media shows, we'll organise more traditional shows, such as Matisse/Picasso, and we will give dynamic new views of our collection. At MoMA QNS we will be able to experiment and try out a lot of ideas before we get into our renovated Manhattan building. Our landmark sculpture garden will be back in place in 2005, and our spaces will be expanded two-fold. Like BALTIC, the renovated MoMA will be very accessible, with cafes, film theatres, and lively exhibition and education programming. Visitors will go through the contemporary part of the collection to get to the historical. Our library and study centres will be state-of-the-art.

I'll close by saying that I've been working with my P.S.1 colleagues on a show from Pam and Dick Kramlich's collection. This collector couple in San Francisco has acquired over forty video installations and a library of artists' videotapes. In the Napa Valley they are building a home designed by Herzog and De Meuron. This is a unique private collection. The Kramlichs are the Henry Frick of the 21st century. They think seriously about their collection as a whole, about the history of installation as an art form, and about preservation. In the future their home will probably become a museum, in the same way that we have the Frick Museum in Manhattan. Now I hope you have lots of questions.

(Audience applause)

RICHARD DEACON:

Thank you Barbara and James. Actually I'd like to start with a question to Barbara. When you started at MoMA you weren't employed as a video curator, presumably?

BARBARA LONDON:

No.

RICHARD DEACON:

And although you're interested in video, or you became interested in video...

BARBARA LONDON:

I became interested in video around the same time I assembled the artists' book collection in the Department of Prints and Illustrated Books. The Museum recognised video as an emerging area of contemporary activity. Everything was new and untried. Artists felt part of a transforming process, and I was exhilarated to participate too.

RICHARD DEACON:

At what point did it become a policy of the Museum to collect?

BARBARA LONDON:

Since 1974 I had been organising video shows for the new, ongoing video exhibition programme. Because I was in the Print Department, it was through that department's acquisition committee that the Museum acquired its first artists' videos in 1975.

RICHARD DEACON:

And at that point was the Museum collecting photographs?

BARBARA LONDON:

We started collecting photographs sometime in the thirties. Photography is an important part of the MoMA collection, which tracks the history of the medium.

RICHARD DEACON:

And so photographs have always been a part of the collection?

BARBARA LONDON:

Yes. Film entered the collection in 1935. The Museum was founded in 1929, and early on our first director, Alfred Barr, had the foresight of acquiring, not only painting and sculpture, prints and illustrated books, drawings, architecture and design, but also photography and film. The experimental film collection includes the work of Maya Deren, Andy Warhol, Michael Snow, Stan Brakhage, among many, many others

RICHARD DEACON (TO JAMES PUTNAM):

I'm not quite clear as to whether the post you have at the British Museum is a curatorial position or a temporary position – but it's a roving brief.

JAMES PUTNAM:

Can't it be a temporary curatorial position?

RICHARD DEACON:

As a kind of agitator within the museum?

JAMES PUTNAM:

Well it's funny. There was this *Evening Standard* article by Louisa Buck about me with the headline 'Maverick at the Museum'. I must say I was a bit ashamed of it at first, because it was the last thing I wanted to be called. But then I kind of got used to it and I thought, 'Well, it's rather good isn't it?' and it is, after all, what I am – let's face it. It's not that I want to change things for the sake of it , but I do want to inject some new vitality into the Museum because I believe it's crucial for its image. So in that sense I do work from within the institution but I do have a lot of respect for it and all my museum colleagues. One of the joys of facilitating artists working in the Museum is to take its curatorial specialists out of their usual historical role and to stimulate their passion for their expertise, which provides enormous inspiration to the artists. I'm also aware that I can't go ahead and do things which are avant garde merely for the sake of it in the Museum. It is essential to respect our visitors, so that everything I do needs to communicate in some way to the general public and not interfere with their normal viewing of the collection. So I have to hit a fine line with what's truly appropriate and strive to achieve as much I can within the limitations of the context, which I find really challenging.

RICHARD DEACON:

But there is some overlap between, for example, that Richard Wentworth installation and the kind of objects that the British Museum would collect for an ethnographic display. You saw the Paolozzi show, 'Lost Magic Kingdoms' at the Museum of Mankind – a lot of the objects he had were not dissimilar from Richard Wentworth's objects although collected in the field, as it were, rather than on the street.

JAMES PUTNAM:

Sure. I mean, it may be interesting or not, but the thing that I particularly want to stress with the programme I'm doing is not about collecting at all, it's very much about artists who want to create things or make things inspired by the Museum rather than for acquiring by the Museum.

RICHARD DEACON:

That was my next question: to what extent the things that you are curating would ever become a part of the collection of a museum?

JAMES PUTNAM:

The Andy Goldsworthy work (in 'Time Machine') was in fact an ephemeral piece, but the photo-work, the C-print, was acquired by the Museum. There was also a Marc Quinn drawing from that show and the colossal Igor Mitoraj bronze sculpture was actually donated by the artist to the museum and is still sited on the forecourt. But they were the only concessions to the work being collected and they were never specially commissioned. Richard Wentworth's work, for instance, was dismantled and dispersed after the show. He very much conceived it as a kind of display that he created and not necessarily as an artwork to be preserved intact: well, it couldn't be kept, obviously, because it incorporated objects from the British Museum's collection. This is all related to a fascinating and topical issue which is something I wanted to bring up in the discussion. I mean, Barbara mentioned the potential problems of collecting and where does it all end, and the whole thing that perhaps I was trying to get across in my book is that the museum and contemporary art are becoming increasingly interwoven. In general, before the sixties, you had to be dead to get your work in a museum and nowadays museum's collect work by young artists. They're striving to preserve the present and we now have works that are being, as it were, 'custom made' for museums. That's a situation that didn't happen before, so we're reaching a stage where are we getting completely overtaken by an obsession to collect everything that a significant artist makes.

RICHARD DEACON:

Is this a moral issue? Are you saying it is immoral to make something for the museum, or is it an observation?

JAMES PUTNAM:

It's an observation. I'm not saying it's good or bad, but I guess it is a potential problem in terms of storage and conservation. Due to lack of exhibition space, do these works end up in packing cases never to be opened again, or as some installation with a little diagram that goes with it, of how to re-install it in years to come?

BARBARA LONDON:

There are many issues around the question. A Sol LeWitt wall drawing can be recreated following the artist's very careful notation. Each installer and each location affects the look of the particular LeWitt drawing. Certain kinds of works are site-specific. At MoMA we have our 'Projects' exhibition series, founded in 1971, and devoted to up-to-the-minute art. Some of that work has been very ephemeral, made more in relation to the architecture and site, and some of it has a physical object that's come out of it. With 'Projects', our mandate has not been to buy those works exhibited in the series – it's been liberating, without pressure. Once in a while we have acquired one of the works. But it's the exception.

RICHARD DEACON:

I didn't know that about moving the Museum to Queens, but it certainly looked like you were treating the museum as the contents – that blue building looked like a kind of enormous vitrine. It certainly did look like you were, whether consciously or not, opening a new vitrine in Queens. There were lots of things I wondered about – whether this was a kind of agit-museum, because putting a museum in Queens would change that situation radically. At the same time you have this box which you are aware is full of contents – architecturally it's not particularly distinguishable from any other kind of store. There seemed to be a whole lot of things that were raised about the museum that were interesting.

BARBARA LONDON:

There are. This is a light industry/warehouse section of Queens. Twenty-five years ago you would have no reason to visit this neighborhood. Now there is MoMA QNS, the Sculpture Center, and P.S.1 around the corner. AMI (the American Museum of the Moving Image), the Nouguchi Museum and Socrates Sculpture Park are nearby too. You can easily get from one to the other following a 'culture map'.

The MoMA QNS building was built as a stapler factory. A comparable museum space would be the Temporary/Contemporary, that MoCA in L.A. opened as they were putting up their new Arata Isozaki-designed museum. It is very possible that MoMA curators will be so happy with the large, dynamic MoMA QNS galleries that we won't forsake them. Originally the building was intended as storage after our 11 West 53rd Street building expansion is completed. While MoMA QNS might look like a big vitrine on the outside, inside it resembles BALTIC – we have these amazing high-ceilinged spaces, which are perfect for contemporary art. The dynamic entrance with curved walls swoops visitors up through specially selected new media artwork and into our shows. The highest ceiling in our old building was 12 feet – much too low for most contemporary work. At MoMA QNS we will be experimenting with projections and up-to-date technology, sometimes commissioning a site-specific work. We will be getting into these questions: if a piece is commissioned and made just for MoMA QNS, and it is fantastic, then perhaps we would acquire the work for the collection.

RICHARD DEACON:

But it seems to me that the Museum of Modern Art in particular, through Alfred Barr's model, is this kind of iconic institution, this model of modernism. It's still hung according to Alfred Barr's model to a greater or lesser extent, although the introduction of new media does rock the boat a little bit. But in terms of its iconic status, if a model is shifted then that's an opportunity to shake the model as well.

BARBARA LONDON:

It's both. Our director Glenn Lowry really wants to shake the model too. We are still very deeply entrenched in modernism, but there's a bit of a shift going on right now.

RICHARD DEACON:

At this point I'm going to throw it open to the audience to find out if we've got any questions – if not, we'll just carry on talking amongst ourselves!

QUESTION:

Are there any plans to digitise the collection to allow works to be viewed on the internet?

BARBARA LONDON:

As you know this involves issues of copyright, and many rights holders see their collections/databases as revenue producing. I work in an institution where my colleagues in the Department of Film and Media feel that film is film. To them, it should never be digitised. They're softening a little bit, just for study purposes. But whatever the millimetre of the film is, you'll always be able to see it the way it was supposed to be seen in our theatre. You'll also be able to see the new media work as well and you'll also be able to hear it the way it was meant to be heard. You won't have a popcorn machine popping when the door opens – you'll have a real state of the art sound, which is what we've always done.

RICHARD DEACON:

But with the Joan Jonas *Vertical Roll* for example, what's the point of showing that on a machine that doesn't have a vertical hold? What the *Vertical Roll* does, as a piece, is transparent: it's both about the medium and the point of transmission. If you transfer that to a display system that doesn't have a vertical hold, you lose that connection.

BARBARA LONDON:

Yes – that piece has a vertical roll built in, and it should be seen on a monitor. I think those works should not be shown on a flat screen because I think Joan, when she made it, was really thinking about the TV box, not a flat screen and not projected. The tape was meant to be on this intimate scale. Currently on view at MoMA we have a show entitled 'First Decade', and it really is the first decade of video. Amazing treasures are being shown. Because 'First Decade' is on while we are closing down our 53rd Street facility, I didn't have a gallery to put that show in. So most of the works are presented in our theatre, but works like Joan's are shown on a monitor in our Education Center.

RICHARD DEACON:

But on the other hand, the things that James has shown us are almost about doing the reverse. They are to do with undermining the display systems of the museum in order to, presumably, give you a way of looking which is non-habitual.

JAMES PUTNAM:

They are in a way. I saw the British Museum as a kind of fertile space for colonising, albeit temporarily with contemporary art, a site which didn't have to conform to the white space aesthetic – where art and artefacts could interact in a really exciting way. I found that many artists I involved in this practice were inspired by the new possibilities it opened up for them. Some of them remarked, 'It's really boring exhibiting in the proverbial white cube. It's really exciting and challenging to do something in this new kind of space and for a different audience than the minority initiated in contemporary art.' But like many of the best things in art it involves risk and could be a disaster both for the artist and the Museum. My point was that because the artists are using that space they have an understanding of it – art and artifact become an integral installation, like Sir John Soane's Museum.

BARBARA LONDON:

I'll just make a quick point that at MoMA we have done a little bit of that. We have an 'Artist's Choice' series, in which Scott Burton re-installed the Brancusi's in our collection, taking away the original plinths. It was quite amazing to see one of the Brancusi heads lying right on the carpeted floor. Chuck Close did an 'Artist's Choice' show of portraits from our collection. He had railing ledges, three rows of them, installed around the periphery of the gallery. The framed print and photographic portraits were set chock-a-block right next to each other, so you saw all these works in a very different way. I think those different views are important, because they shake up the curatorial thinking and open things up.

JAMES PUTNAM:

It keeps a kind of fluidity within the space. I think that question of, does the work change when it gets museum-ified, does it lose some of its quality, maybe Richard, as an artist, can say something about that?

RICHARD DEACON (TO JAMES PUTNAM):

What I was going to say was that what you said seemed to be the artist's point of view, but actually the question would be, what does it do to the artifacts? Scott Burton was very heavily criticised and I've done things like that as well – I put a carpet under a David Smith sculpture, which was very heavily criticised at the time. I've just worked on the show at the Tate ('Image and Idol: Medieval Sculpture', Tate Britain, September – March 2002) where I brought things in and tried to work on the things you put underneath other objects as a means of trying to show them in a different way. But I guess the question would be, what does the Andy Goldsworthy do for the Egyptian objects? I mean, it works well with the space but what does it do for the Egyptian objects?

JAMES PUTNAM:

I think, visually, it did do something for the rest of the collection. Funnily enough, when we installed it some people reacted in horror saying, 'you can't bring sand into the Museum!' But the fact is that all these Egyptian sculptures were excavated from the sand so in a sense, it brought more context to them. After all, everything in a museum's out of context anyway. I think it did link the ancient sculpture together in a really nice way, perhaps suggesting the serpentine form of the River Nile. But there again this work was only in there for about three days because some people would have complained about access to viewing the sculpture. It was also a through route so there were issues of health and safety, fire exits, etc. But in retrospect, its very ephemerality was its strength and completely in character with the artist's work. It also provided us with a dynamic image for our exhibition poster.

QUESTION:

I have a completely horrible question for Barbara. But actually it was James' use of the word 'colonising' that sort of struck up this chain of thought. As I'm sure you know, there are ways of looking at MoMA outside of the United States that are critical of the kind of track through the recent past that is created by this wonderful institution. Now I'm thinking of the problem in this country of the fact that there is no collection anywhere of the first decade of video art – absolutely nobody knows anything about it but, it happened here. So in this sense, this country is as unknown as Africa, the Middle East, Korea or all these places that are now very trendy for curating exhibitions and welcoming artists from. But isn't it ironic that Europe is so little known in terms of its own recent history? And I wondered, looking at that from your point of view, if you had anything that you could say to allow people here to contextualise their own work, not within an American history since it's only the American history that's known?

BARBARA LONDON:

Based upon the little bits I know, I would hope that a place like the Tate or some institution in Great Britain will accept some of these archives and start to deal with preservation. Today I was at Locus+ and saw Jon Bewley and Simon Herbert and they were talking about their archives. At a certain point somebody trashed a lot of their ephemeral materials, which were thrown out accidentally – a real pity.

QUESTION:

But isn't it too late to go back and collect video tapes from the seventies?

BARBARA LONDON:

No, it's not too late. You'd be surprised. Often the most gummed up tapes retain their original information, which is revealed after cleaning.

QUESTION:

Well, do you think artists have kept their reel-to-reel videos?

BARBARA LONDON:

I think a lot of artists have.

RICHARD DEACON:

I have!

BARBARA LONDON:

This is something for the Arts Council to support. The community here has to lobby for funds. You don't have to take it all on at once. That's what we've done at MoMA – we have this collection of over a thousand titles, which we're adding to all the time. We have a long tradition at MoMA of film preservation. A year and a half ago we obtained an NEA grant for video preservation, and we bit off a manageable piece of the pie to preserve. The project is being completed this last year. I look at this year's preservation as one chapter. At the same time, we went to a foundation to help Carolee Schneeman preserve several of her early films. You must begin somewhere, then you do the report and apply for another grant. I'm preparing a planning grant at MoMA to preserve the Gary Hill and Taiji Furuhashi works I just showed, because very few people are even thinking about the future of video installations.

RICHARD DEACON:

A part of the problem is that the format changes so fast that if you don't preserve it within a reasonable period of time, then the thing disappears. And if the thing disappears, you lose history. It's quite possible for Vermeer to fall foul of fashion, but the paintings don't disappear. And two hundred years later, the Vermeer's start to move up with people's interest in them. The problem, really, is to do with rapid turnover of formats and that where an institution has an active collecting, promoting, storing and archiving policy, that history becomes the only history – which to me is quite a serious issue.

QUESTION

Just on a point of information: these problems with regard to the history of British video are currently being very much discussed. My colleague as was – he's now gone to Central St. Martin's – Nick Curtis, has not only published a great deal on this but he's also running and has set up a research institute at Central St. Martin's to deal precisely with this area of practice. There are, of course, huge problems with a lot of work which is not in a public collection. A lot of it is copied and Central St. Martin's now has a growing archive and the Lux collection, of course, is being looked after. So the issues are very current and they are being discussed.

RICHARD DEACON:

And it's not just an art issue. It relates to the history of science and political history as well. If you can't actually access the protocols for nuclear response in the fifties, then a whole aspect of that history is lost.

COMMENT FROM AUDIENCE:

I am aware of all these things, truly I am, but it's not the same as the Museum of Modern Art providing a kind of basic history against which all other histories are inevitably measured. I don't know of a history of British video art that isn't full of holes because the material just isn't around any more for anyone to find. It probably isn't a great tragedy in any sense, but it creates a kind of imbalance for younger artists working now with the kind of models that they look at.

RICHARD DEACON:

But isn't that a part of what James has just been saying about the museumification of the world? We could preserve everything. Do we actually want to preserve everything? Aren't you happy to forget?

QUESTION:

Aren't things initially made to be temporary anyway? Some installations are about the ephemeral and the temporary and to try to preserve them or recreate them seems to be almost like a contradiction in terms – almost like you're trying to save something that wasn't meant to be, and cannot be, saved anyway.

BARBARA LONDON:

Some works are meant to be saved and can be. Perhaps some are meant to wither away and remain in the viewer's memory.

QUESTION:

It's like when you see a Joseph Beuys reconstructed, you know, you get the feeling that everything's slightly in the wrong place – the context of the symbolism is changed and there's all sorts of other readings going on.

BARBARA LONDON:

I agree. The line needs to be drawn somewhere. I've seen early Japanese Gutai performances recreated and it was dreadful. It's better that there be five written reports with five people's viewing experiences than to have that horrific reproduction, which gives the young generation a flawed view of what the work is about.

RICHARD DEACON:

Edward Allington always had a very nice fantasy on this theme to do with the Argonaut: that the Argonaut was only ever repaired with new parts and over the last two and a half millennia, the Argonaut had been continuously repaired and was now a tourist shop in Athens, which I always thought was very a beautiful idea! Another question you could ask – I put it out to people who are perhaps producers – do you want to remember everything or are you happy to forget? And can the museum also help you to forget as well as to remember? Actually that would be a good question to both of you!

QUESTION:

That question is relevant with regard to the show at MoMA of photographs of the streets of New York. Do we need to remember that, up to the moment that the twin towers were blown up – do we need to see those kinds of photos again – or can we move on and leave them forgotten? With the kind of work we're talking about here, if you digitise it, then you don't need to keep the physical artifacts.

BARBARA LONDON:

This is very complicated. Days after 9.11, a non-profit storefront was set up in Soho on Prince Street, where they accepted and put up images of the twin towers and the event. The photos were by very famous journalists, as well as the ordinary mortal. You could go in and buy a print for $25, and the money went to the relief fund. My institution's show and the storefront show are part of the healing process. It is valid... then we move on with our lives.

JAMES PUTNAM:

I was going to say that, certainly as far as museums are concerned, the artifacts themselves do represent a kind of material evidence – the verification of facts via artifacts. Everything that a museum collects, however it's interpreted later on, is read as evidence and provides a basis for future research, subsequently published in academic papers. Therefore what has been collected is a form of cultural history of that time. Unfortunately – or fortunately, as the case may be – there's always this argument where people say, 'Some of these so-called important artists will be forgotten in years to come – they're merely flavour of the month'. But the fact is, they are represented in international collections and they have been acquired because they are believed by some to represent historically the culture of that time. They'll remain in public collections for posterity – in this country you can't de-accession anything that's in a public collection. In America I know it's different – you can sell off museum objects, can't you?

BARBARA LONDON:

Yes. There are different rules and regulations. Alfred Barr, our first director – he was quite an amazing man – created departments of painting and sculpture, prints and illustrated books, and drawings, and then he added film and photography, as well as architecture and design departments before any other museum of modern art. But he also said, 'In the long run, if I am 2 per cent right in my acquisition decisions, I will have been a success.' (To James) And it really is your point: if it's in the collection, if there was a knowledgeable curator who went to bat for it, and it's not my speciality, well, who am I to say? So things get pulled out of the storeroom and get put on the wall and taken off the wall. This is taste, and the pressures of the time, and it will always, always happen.

RICHARD DEACON:

That's the benefit of the collection, you see: you put stuff in store and maybe someone else will want it. The Tate has stuff in store that's never going to come out and it has made mistakes as well as inspired guesses. My question was, can museums ever make you forget? The answer is yes, they can make you forget – and this is exactly Susan's point. For example, if it had only preserved non-paper artefacts then we'd have a very different view of history, or we'd construct a very different view of material history. But also the museum is not passive, it acts actively, which goes back to the question of MoMA's role in Queens: the museum is being proactive in Queens in a way that it hasn't been before and wasn't originally. The 'Art of Our Time' logo was a very proactive installation. Is it going to have 'Art of Our Time' on the new building?

BARBARA LONDON:

Not exactly in that way! We are planning a range of celebratory works for the opening in Queens. Later this spring, Francis Alÿs will orchestrate a pageant from Manhattan to Queens. And Tsai Quo Chan will to do one of his firework pieces. It is important that New York has more than one museum presenting contemporary art. There's MoMA, the Guggenheim, the Whitney and there are smaller museums, such as the Grey Art Gallery and the New Museum – of course the latter doesn't have a collection. The different points of view mean a range of new work gets shown, and we need that dialogue.

JAMES PUTNAM:

I have to say one thing about that 'forgotten' question. There are some works of art that are forgotten, but there are some that have some kind of rumour about them that almost makes them more powerful in a sense – all these lost paintings that are then recovered, for example. So I think sometimes not having the artifact can be even more powerful.

QUESTION:

I think this question of forgetting is really interesting. (To Barbara) Even within your talk you had this slide of what was a Nam June Paik coloured piece, but from my memory there was an interactive colour organ done by another artist who was at the Museum of Modern Art but he's forgotten. So even within the Museum of Modern Art there are ways of killing off people who don't fit into the canon, which is exactly what Susan's question was.

BARBARA LONDON:

Many works from many different camps are made at one time. Some are in the limelight and some not, and a canon forms. It is important to consider what is in the shadows, outside the system. Some of these works are re-evaluated and moved to the centre, with the next generation or before.

At MoMA we had two important shows that included a lot of now obscure artists. 'The Machine as Seen at the

End of the Mechanical Age' (1968) show, organized by Pontus Hultén, began with a drawing by Leonardo of a 'flying machine' and concluded with a view into the future in the form of Nam June Paik's videos. Another show, 'Information' (1970) caught conceptual art at its start.

QUESTION:

It's a big question really that we might want to think about over a drink, but is there ever any argument for preserving a whole museum?

RICHARD DEACON:

Yes. Museums are preserved. I can give you one example straight off: the Natural History Museum in Dublin. The installation of the exhibits in the Natural History Museum in Dublin is preserved as an installation as well as a working natural history museum. The Sir John Soane (London) would be another example, as would the Pitt Rivers Museum (Oxford), which is a very important museum to have conserved.

QUESTION:

Is this argument going to arise at all in the future of MoMA? You were saying how deeply it was embedded in modernism. Quite apart from die-hard people refusing to change, is there an argument for saying, 'Just keep it and we'll start again in Queens on the riverbank'?

RICHARD DEACON:

That's not a bad idea!

BARBARA LONDON:

We are changing. At MoMA QNS a portion of the collection will be installed in a radically different way. It's a start.

RICHARD DEACON:

Another example is the Winckelmann Room in the British Museum, downstairs: the installation of the classical sculptures.

BARBARA LONDON:

When you come to New York, go to the Natural History Museum and look at the North Coast Indian room installed by the anthropologist Franz Boas in the early 20th century. It's unbelievable when you consider colonialism and anthropology; what anthropology is and what another culture is. Boas' wall labels make references to good and evil in ways we wouldn't today.

QUESTION (TO JAMES PUTNAM):

I'm trying to deal with museums being static but it seems that museums have changed quite a lot in the past two years. How has that affected the way you're thinking about curating now?

JAMES PUTNAM:

It's changed slightly for the worse from my point of view because I haven't been able to do any more intervention shows at the Museum. Actually, having used the word 'intervention', I didn't think the word intervention constituted an exhibition, but I have to put all my projects before an exhibitions committee and none of them have got accepted – so I've almost given up! I thought, 'Well I've got to try and do other things that don't involve that.' But interestingly enough, I have seen that the Great Court, which is this new, Norman Foster-designed space within the British Museum, is somewhat different in that it's kind of a public space and it doesn't come under the remit of the curatorial control of the various keepers of the departments. There is a possibility to try and create interventions there. So, last week in fact, when we were doing this conference called 'From Material Things', we had a work by a young Canadian artist called Germaine Koh which was an 80-metre long knitwork that we just unravelled down the staircase of the Great Court. I had asked the permission of senior management and no one responded. So I wasn't sure whether we were allowed to do it or not: I think we were probably officially granted permission to install it for maybe two or three hours but no one complained, so we extended it as a performance for a few days. My colleagues seemed to like it and it was, after all, the first contemporary work in that space, so hopefully it's possible to do more.

RICHARD DEACON:

I went to the 'Unknown Amazon' show of recent excavations in the lower Amazon Delta of some very interesting objects. One of the curious aspects of that was that in the Great Court itself there were a group of ethnic Indians making and selling basketworks, which raised interesting questions about the place of vanishing communities within the Museum. (To James) You may have a comment on that, I don't know. They were not exhibits, but they were curiously picturesque in a way which is difficult, though the objects that they made were themselves materially very interesting. The Museum has pushed itself into an area where lots of significant questions are raised.

JAMES PUTNAM:

I must say there is a tendency for some of the British Museum departments to adopt a rather ethnographic approach to collecting contemporary art which is influenced by the restraints imposed by their historical collections. For instance, the Japanese Department might exhibit a lacquer screen or a wood-block print by a contemporary Japanese artist working within that tradition, but would be unlikely to exhibit a work by an artist like Tatsuo Miyajima using electronics or new media. Thus the existing collection often justifies acquisition of art that reflects continuity of tradition rather than major works of contemporary art. Sometimes the Museum will collect ethnographic objects that weren't necessarily meant to be preserved, because they have a remit to collect from disappearing cultures. Then it gets on to the question of how important or indeed appropriate is it to collect them? It's a very interesting question.

RICHARD DEACON:

And it brings us back to the question about British video art of the seventies.

QUESTION (SUSAN HILLER):

I admit to an obsession with museums these days, one I think most artists share. We do live within a culture that tends to museumify everything and I just think that one of the debates that must be relevant to all of this is, are we collecting ourselves in this kind of exercise and turning ourselves into exhibits?

JAMES PUTNAM:

But as an artist, do you aspire to have your work in a museum? Is that a reason for making work?

SUSAN HILLER:

Some work, but other work would be totally inappropriate to be preserved or documented. The tragedy of that approach is that if you look at the history of the past, we only know what sort of vessels and jewellery and weapons people had; we don't know anything about their songs or their conversation or much about their recipes or food. And it's the same thing – if a lot of artists are making work in those ephemeral areas that are inappropriate to document or collect, then again it doesn't get passed forward in any way. These are very interesting issues, I think, for artists to consider.

JAMES PUTNAM:

And would some artists like to have their work in museums – in an archive, for example – but not shown? I'd like to say that although the British Museum is not an art museum as such, it does have some art objects in there, but it's very much in order to represent the culture. They can be everyday objects or artifacts, all kinds of things, so it's not saying, 'this is the Museum of Fine Art.' In fact, some of its utilitarian artifacts are far more interesting than a lot of the artwork. Maybe they can be reappraised as being 'artwork'. I think if we looked at the 'Africa 95' exhibition, which covered thousands of years of African history, some of the most aesthetically appealing objects in there for me were those pre-dynastic ancient Egyptian flint knives and pre-dynastic pottery, which was absolutely incredible. By no stretch of the imagination would they be in the same class as a piece of Egyptian sculpture but they still had their own statement, their own power as great works, in a sense.

QUESTION:

In terms of your curatorial practice, you both talked a lot about how bringing artists into your museums has caused you, as curators, to rethink the way you collect and archive, and to rethink taxonomies. For example, if you think about Richard Wentworth's coke bottles and how that has related to the writing of labels, or about how wanting to see Joan Jonas's work on a monitor has caused you rethink the taxonomy of the media. But I'd be interested to hear you say more about how bringing artists into your museums has caused, not only your curatorial colleagues, but your other colleagues in say, marketing or education, to rethink ideas of exhibition display.

BARBARA LONDON:

You used the words 'marketing' and 'education'. MoMA has always been curatorially driven, and when we did our website it was curatorially driven. It's not market driven. Certainly we need advertising and we need promotion to get the word out about shows and about work, but I really look at marketing as being something that works with us. My museum, whether we like it or not, is still curatorially driven. Unfortunately, in all North American museums, education is the low 'person' on the totem pole, although we do think a lot about our viewers, and always try to provide a context so that neophytes have a hook and feel comfortable about their own interpretations.

COMMENT FROM AUDIENCE:

It's just the sceptic in me who thinks about museums as always under this constant pressure to bring more people through the door. I specifically remember seeing the Pollock show at MoMA and as you stepped out of the exhibition you were confronted with a bank of computers that were displaying a virtual CD.

BARBARA LONDON:

This is an age old problem, that people are going to come for Picasso, they're going to come for Pollock, and now that Bill Viola has become more of a name, they might turn out in numbers for him.

JAMES PUTNAM:

I would think that, if one followed Alfred Barr's original mission statement, the whole of the Museum of Modern Art is completely market driven – it's like a production line, the torpedo through time thing. He saw everything as a means of production, whether it was the exhibition or the book in the shop. Wasn't that his whole philosophy?

BARBARA LONDON:

I think he saw it as a whole entity, yes. But he was really thinking about the collection, more than anything, when he used that model.

RICHARD DEACON:

Was his torpedo armed? In his imagination, was this torpedo destined to hit something? It's a strange analogy to use; it's an update of an arrow through time, but I always imagine that a torpedo is armed.

BARBARA LONDON:

He was aiming it at the future. It was right after World War 1 when he used the metaphor, but he wasn't thinking about warfare.

RICHARD DEACON:

OK. So we'll take one more question.

QUESTION (TO BARBARA LONDON):

Maybe it's a question that's been asked before, but I have the phrase 'entrenched in modernism' stuck in my head. I was just wondering if you foresee, or if the Museum foresees, a point when it becomes the Museum of Twentieth Century Art and how you somehow ascertain or guarantee your relationship to the contemporary as a museum. Or at some point do you say, 'OK, we're a museum of that period?'

BARBARA LONDON

The fact that my museum is expanding shows we're very committed to the 21st century. Our Department of Film and Media, which I'm in, is moving along, as are my colleagues in Painting and Sculpture. There's a really strong mandate to acquire contemporary work and to show it.

RICHARD DEACON

OK. I'd just like to thank Barbara and James for having come through this and thank you all for coming.

(Audience applause)

SPEAKERS' BIOGRAPHIES

ANDREW BURTON

Andrew Burton is head of the Department of Fine Art and Lecturer in Sculpture at the University of Newcastle. He is a sculptor who has produced a number of major public commissions including *Annunciation*, commissioned by Sculpture at Goodwood (2000) and *Cycle*, commissioned by Dudley Metropolitan Borough Council (2001). He has had solo exhibitions at venues including the Herbert Gallery, Coventry (2000) and the European Ceramics Work Centre in the Netherlands (1996).

SACHA CRADDOCK

Sacha Craddock, an independent art critic, teaches at numerous art colleges, writes articles and catalogue essays and gives public lectures. The chair of 'New Contemporaries', she is in the process of setting up *Monitor*, a publication that will establish a forum for critical writing, discussion and newly commissioned work. She is also involved in establishing the Brighton International Photo Biennial 2003 and co-curates, with three others, the new Bloomberg Space in the City of London.

RICHARD DEACON

Richard Deacon is one of Britain's most significant contemporary sculptors and a member of the Board of Trustees for BALTIC. He has exhibited extensively both in the UK and internationally. His work is represented in many public collections both in this country and elsewhere. He has made commissioned work in England, France, Germany, Switzerland, Canada, Japan, China and New Zealand. Deacon has been Visiting Professor at Chelsea School of Art and the London Institute since 1992 and Professor at Ecole Nationale Superieure des Beaux Arts, Paris, since 1999.

LAURA GODFREY-ISAACS

Laura Godfrey-Isaacs is an artist, curator and academic. She trained as a painter at the Slade School of Art and in New York, on a Fulbright Fellowship. In 1998 she ceased her practice as an artist and set up the art organisation HOME, which is based inside her own family house in Camberwell, London. HOME works collaboratively with a range of international artists who realise exhibitions, performances, events, talks and workshops from within the functioning spaces of her house. HOME is a major research project and consultancy, which investigates the relationship between contemporary art and the domestic.

SUSAN HILLER

Artist Susan Hiller holds the BALTIC Chair in Contemporary Art at the University of Newcastle. She uses cultural artefacts as basic materials to investigate themes such as language, belief, desire and the subconscious mind. Some of Susan Hiller's work can be seen currently in 'Self-Evident' at Tate Britain, 'Real Life' at Tate St. Ives. and 'Taster' at the DAAD Gallery, Berlin. A solo exhibition of her recent installations using sound, video and the internet is now at the Museet fur Samidskunst, Roskilde, Denmark. Other recent exhibitions in which she has participated include the Sydney Biennale (2002) and the Bienale de Habana (2001).

BARBARA LONDON

Barbara London is a curator in the Department of Film and Media at The Museum of Modern Art in New York. She founded the Museum's ongoing new media exhibition programme, creating a platform for artists such as Laurie Anderson, Gary Hill, Joan Jonas, Nam June Paik and Bill Viola, working in the then-emerging media of video and electronic art. She established the Video

Study Center at MoMA to document and preserve work in this field. As a curator at MoMA she has organised numerous exhibitions including 'Video Spaces: Eight Installations' (1995) and 'The First Decade: Video from the EAI Archives' (2002). Barbara London has written widely on video and media art, and her curatorial dispatches from Russia, Ukraine, China, and Japan have been published on the MoMA website. (www.moma.org/onlineprojects)

JOHN MILNER

John Milner is Professor of Art History at the University of Newcastle. His numerous publications include studies on the art of the early Soviet period (*Kazimir Malevich and the Art of Geometry*, 1996, and *A Dictionary of Russian and Soviet Artists*, 1993) and on late nineteenth-century Paris in *The Studios of Paris: The Capital of Art in the Late Nineteenth Century* (1988). More recently he has published *Art, War and Revolution: France 1870-1871* (2000).

JAMES PUTNAM

James Putnam is founder and curator of the Contemporary Arts & Cultures Programme at the British Museum, London, where he has staged a number of innovative exhibitions. In 1994 he curated the exhibition 'Time Machine: Ancient Egypt and Contemporary Art', in which works by contemporary artists such as Marc Quinn and Andy Goldsworthy were displayed within the Museum's Egyptian Galleries. He also acts as an independent curator and has been working on an ongoing series of exhibitions at the Freud Museum, London. James Putnam has written a number of publications on both the history of ancient Egypt and contemporary art, including *Art and Artifact: The Museum as Medium* (Thames and Hudson, 2001).

DR ANDREW RENTON

Dr Andrew Renton is the Slade Curator at the Slade School of Fine Art, University College London, and an independent curator and writer. He has curated numerous international exhibitions and was co-curator for Manifesta 1, the first European Biennial in Rotterdam in 1996. He was also co-curator of 'Browser' (Vancouver, 1997), a project involving 350 artists, another version of which was made for the Tate Gallery, London, in 2000 ('Bankside Browser'). More recently, he curated the exhibition 'Total Object Complete with Missing Parts' at Tramway, Glasgow (2001). Dr Renton has published widely on contemporary art, including *Technique Anglaise: Current Trends in British Art* (Thames & Hudson, 1991), and writes a weekly column on contemporary art issues in the *Evening Standard* newspaper.

JONATHAN WATKINS

Jonathan Watkins joined Ikon in Birmingham as director in autumn 1999, following his appointment as artistic director of the 11th Sydney Biennale. Previously he worked for a number of years with major galleries in London, as curator of the Serpentine (1995-97) and director of Chisenhale Gallery (1990-95). As a guest curator, Jonathan Watkins has contributed to 'Quotidiana', Castello di Rivoli, Turin (1999-2000) and 'Europarte', La Biennale di Venezia (1997). He was British commissioner for 'Milano Europa 2000', Palazzo di Triennale, Milan and guest curator for 'Facts of Life': an exhibition of contemporary Japanese art at the Hayward Gallery, London (2001). He is also guest curator for the forthcoming Tate Triennial at Tate Britain (Spring 2003).